easy **GUITAR EDITION**

The Best EASY Book of
Christmas Guitar

Over 100 Christmas Favorites, Plus a Special Easy Solo Guitar TAB Section!

Copyright © MMVIII by Alfred Publishing Co., Inc.
All rights reserved. Printed in USA.

ISBN-10: 0-7390-5525-9
ISBN-13: 978-0-7390-5525-0

Cover Photos
Cabin in the snow: © Milan Vasicek / Dreamstime.com • Sky: © istockphoto / Online Creative Media

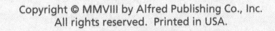

Contents

BONUS GUITAR SOLO SECTION

ALL I WANT FOR CHRISTMAS IS MY TWO FRONT TEETH

Words and Music by
DON GARDENER

ANGELS FROM THE REALMS OF GLORY

Words by
JOHN MONTGOMERY

Music by
HENRY SMART

Verse 3:
Sages, leave your contemplations,
Brighter visions beam afar.
Seek the great desire of nations,
Ye have seen His natal star.
(To Chorus:)

ANGELS WE HAVE HEARD ON HIGH

TRADITIONAL FRENCH CAROL

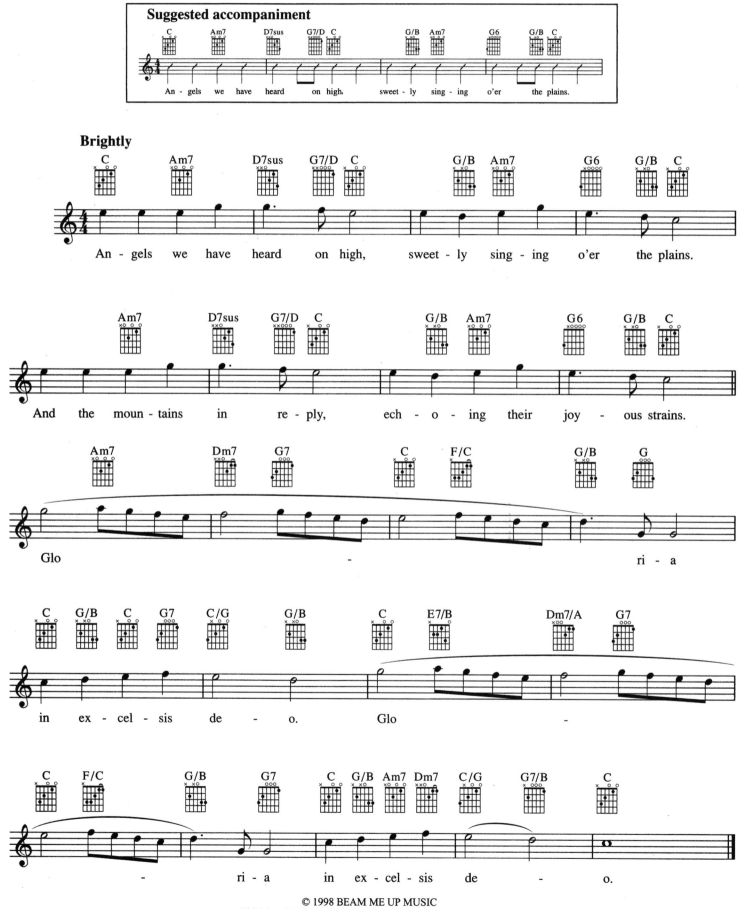

AS LATELY WE WATCHED

TRADITIONAL

Verse 3:
His throne is a manger, His court is a loft.
But troops of bright angels, in lay, sweet and soft.
Him they proclaim, our Christ by name.
And earth, sky and air, straight are filled with His fame.

Verse 4:
Then shepherds, be joyful, salute your liege King.
Let hills and dales ring to the song that ye sing.
Blest be the hour, welcome the morn.
For Christ our dear Savior on earth now is born.

AULD LANG SYNE

Words by
ROBERT BURNS

TRADITIONAL
SCOTTISH AIR

AWAY IN A MANGER

Words by
MARTIN LUTHER

Music by
J.E. SPILLAN

A BABE IS BORN IN BETHLEHEM

Words and Music by
LUDWIG LINDEMAN

Verse 3:
The wise men came, led by the star,
Gold, myrrh, and incense brought from far.
Alleluia, alleluia.

Verse 4:
On this most blessed jubilee, blest jubilee,
All glory be, O God, to Thee.
Alleluia, alleluia.

THE BABE

Translated by
BERNARD GASSO

TRADITIONAL MEXICAN

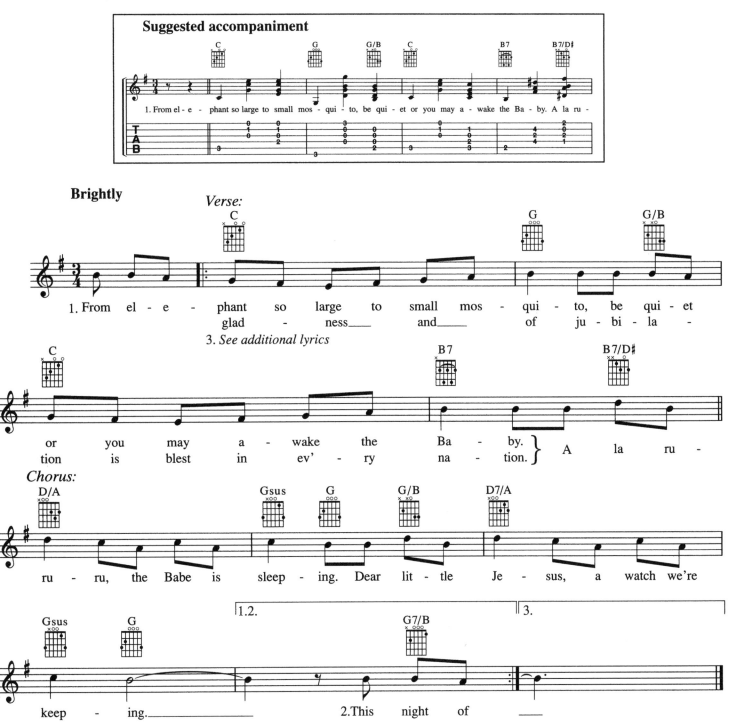

Brightly

Verse:

1. From el - e - phant so large to small mos - qui - to, be qui - et
glad - ness_____ and_____ of ju - bi - la -

3. See additional lyrics

or you may a - wake the Ba - by.
tion is blest in ev' - ry na - tion. } A la ru -

Chorus:

ru - ru, the Babe is sleep - ing. Dear lit - tle Je - sus, a watch we're

keep - ing._____
2. This night of _____

Verse 3:
Celestial voices, in sweet accents singing,
The wondrous tidings of His birth are bringing.
(To Chorus:)

THE BELLS OF CHRISTMAS

Words and Music by
MARY STUART

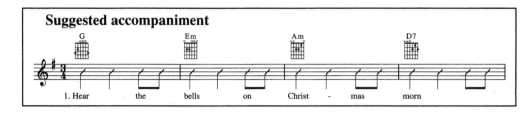

Moderate waltz

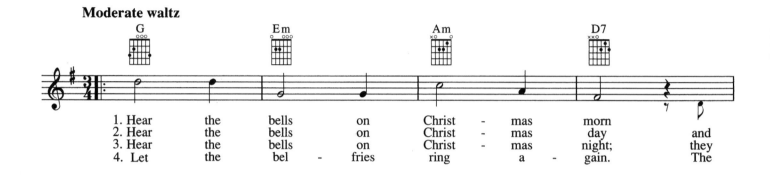

1. Hear the bells on Christ - mas morn
2. Hear the bells on Christ - mas day and
3. Hear the bells on Christ - mas night; they
4. Let the bel - fries ring a - gain. The

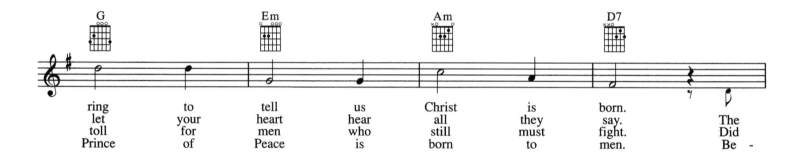

ring to tell us Christ is born. The
let your heart hear all they say. The
toll for men who still must fight. Did
Prince of Peace is born to men. Be -

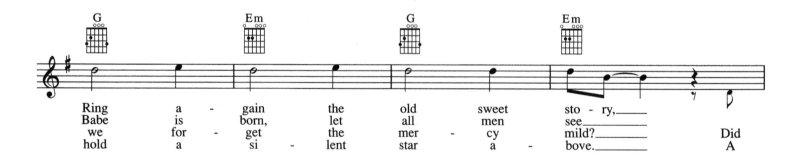

Ring a - gain the old sweet sto - ry,_____
Babe is born, let all men see_____
we for - get the mer - cy mild?_____ Did
hold a si - lent star a - bove._____ A

To Coda ⊕

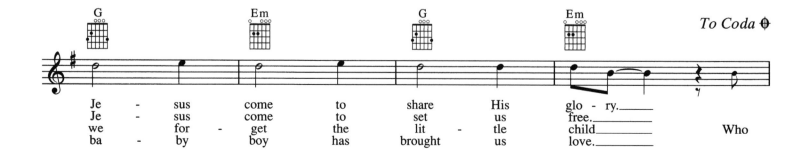

Je - sus come to share His glo - ry._____
Je - sus come to set us free._____
we for - get the lit - tle child_____ Who
ba - by boy has brought us love._____

The Bells of Christmas - 2 - 1

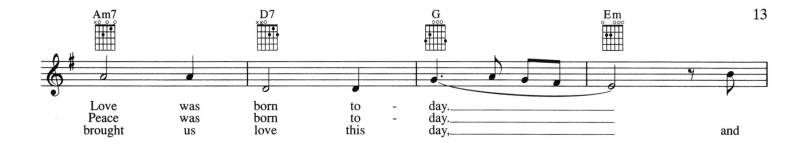

Love   was   born   to - day._____
Peace   was   born   to - day._____
brought us   love   this day,_____   and

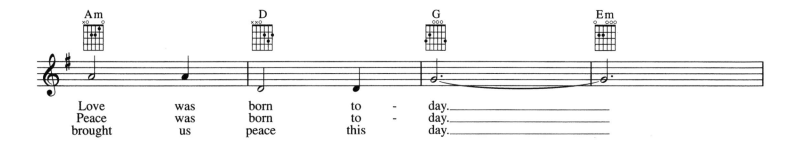

Love   was   born   to - day._____
Peace   was   born   to - day._____
brought us   peace   this day._____

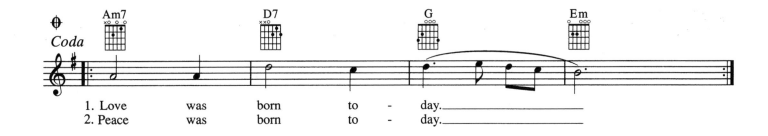

1.2. |3.   *D.C. al Coda*

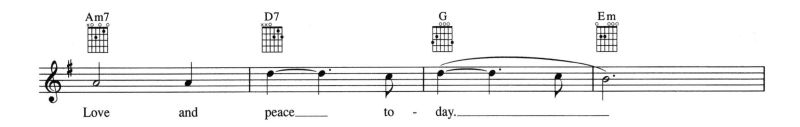

Coda

1. Love   was   born   to - day._____
2. Peace was   born   to - day._____

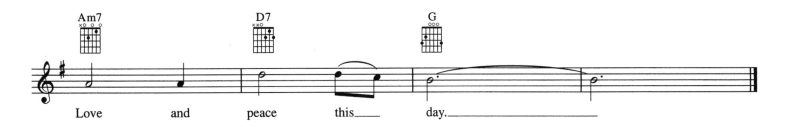

Love   and   peace_____ to - day._____

Love   and   peace   this_____ day._____

THE BOAR'S HEAD CAROL

ANCIENT OXFORD CAROL
XVI CENTURY

BORN IS HE, THIS HOLY CHILD

FRENCH CAROL

Verse 3:
Jesus, Thou all-powered Lord.
Now as Baby art Thou adored.
Jesus, Thou all-powered King.
All our hearts to Thee we bring.
(To Chorus:)

BRIGHT AND JOYFUL IS THE MORN

Words by
JAMES MONTGOMERY

WELSH HYMN

BRING A TORCH, JEANETTE, ISABELLA

TRADITIONAL FRENCH

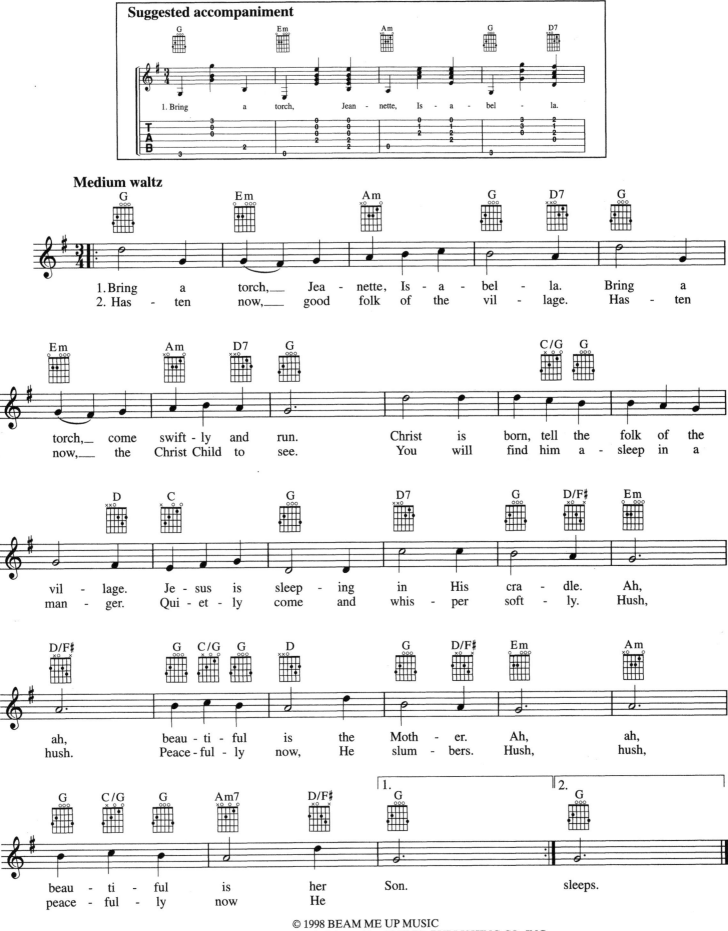

CAROL OF THE BIRDS

TRADITIONAL

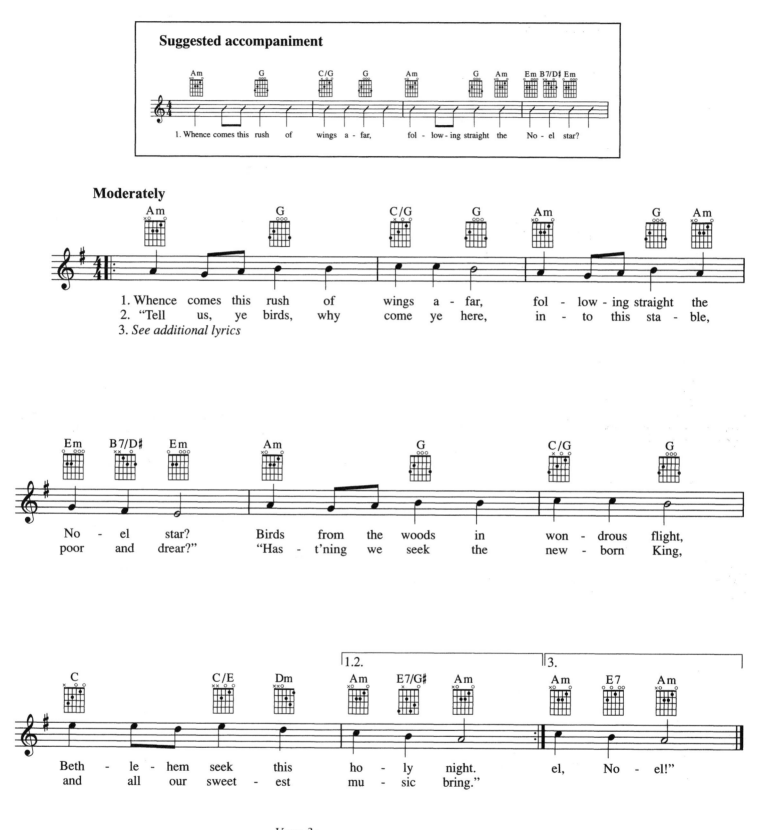

Verse 3:
Angels and shepherds, birds of the sky,
Come where the Son of God doth lie.
Christ on earth with man doth dwell,
Join in the shout, "Noel, Noel!"

A CHILD THIS DAY IS BORN

TRADITIONAL

Brightly *Verse:*

1. A child this day is___ born, a child of high___ re - nown, most
ti - dings shep - herds___ heard. In field watch - ing___ their fold were

3. See additional lyrics

wor - thy of a scep - tre, a scep - tre and a crown. } No -
by an an - gel un - to them that night re - vealed and told.

Chorus:

el, No - el, No - el, No - el, sing all___ we may be - cause the King of

all_____ kings was born this bless - ed day. { 2. These   day.
3. And

Verse 3:
And as the angel told them,
So to them did appear.
They found the young Child, Jesus Christ,
With Mary, his Mother dear.
(To Chorus:)

CHRIST WAS BORN ON CHRISTMAS DAY

TRADITIONAL AMERICAN

Verse 3:
Let the bright red berries glow,
Everywhere in goodly show.
Christus natus hodie,
The Babe, the Son,
The Holy One of Mary.

Verse 4:
Christian men, rejoice and sing,
'Tis the birthday of a King.
Ex Maria Virgine,
The God, the Lord,
By all adorned forever.

THE COVENTRY CAROL

TRADITIONAL ENGLISH CAROL

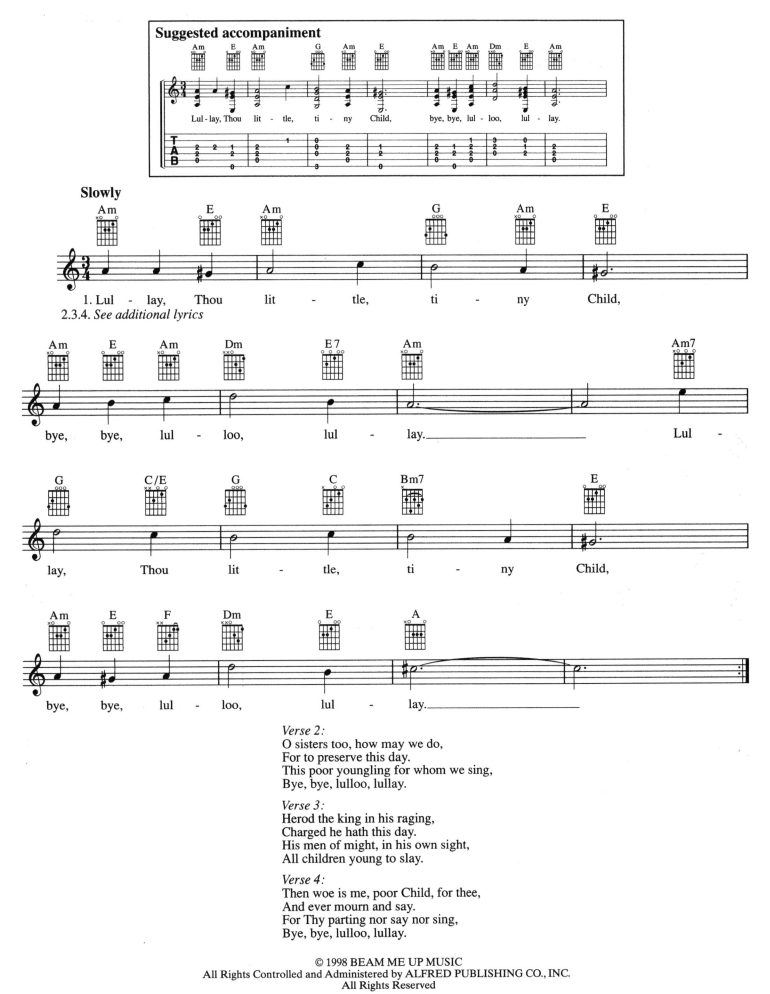

Verse 2:
O sisters too, how may we do,
For to preserve this day.
This poor youngling for whom we sing,
Bye, bye, lulloo, lullay.

Verse 3:
Herod the king in his raging,
Charged he hath this day.
His men of might, in his own sight,
All children young to slay.

Verse 4:
Then woe is me, poor Child, for thee,
And ever mourn and say.
For Thy parting nor say nor sing,
Bye, bye, lulloo, lullay.

CHRISTMAS IN KILLARNEY

Words and Music by
JOHN REDMOND, JAMES CAVANAUGH
and FRANK WELDON

Christmas in Killarney - 2 - 1

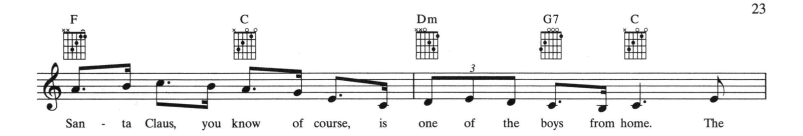

Santa Claus, you know of course, is one of the boys from home. The

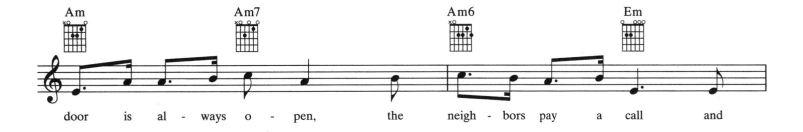

door is al - ways o - pen, the neigh - bors pay a call and

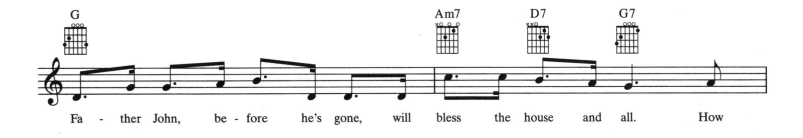

Fa - ther John, be - fore he's gone, will bless the house and all. How

grand it feels, to click your heels, and join in the fun of the jigs and reels. I'm

hand - ing you no blar - ney, the likes you've nev - er known, is Christ-mas in Kil-lar - ney, with

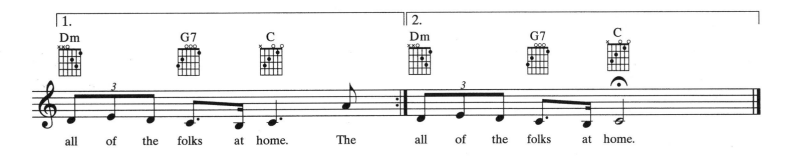

1.
all of the folks at home. The

2.
all of the folks at home.

Christmas in Killarney - 2 - 2

CHRISTMAS IN THE CITY

Words and Music by
JAY LEONHART

Christmas in the City - 2 - 1

THE CHRISTMAS WALTZ

Words by
SAMMY CAHN

Music by
JULE STYNE

DANCE OF THE SUGAR-PLUM FAIRY

Music by
PETER ILYICH TCHAIKOVSKY

Up-tempo two-beat

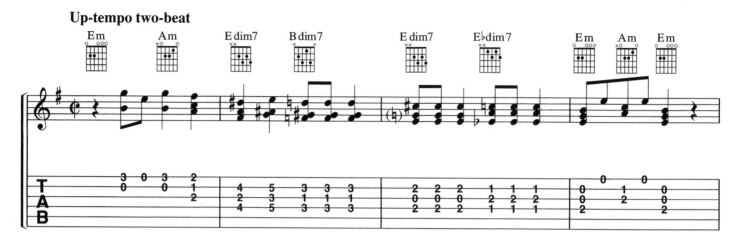

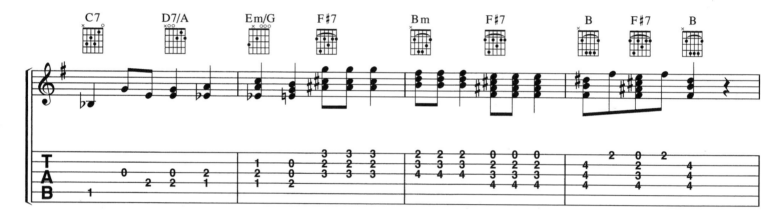

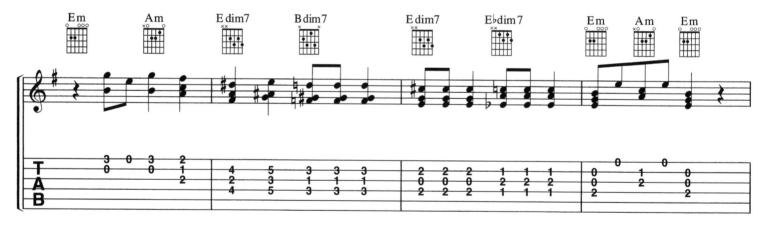

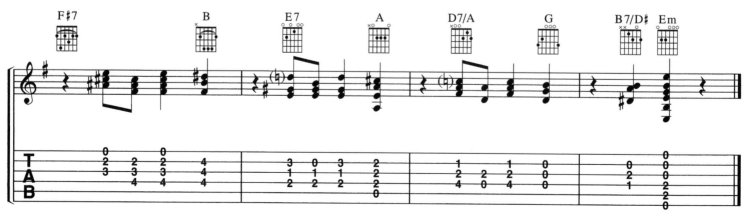

DECK THE HALL

TRADITIONAL OLD WELSH

EMMANUEL

Words and Music by
JANIS IAN and KYE FLEMING

THE FIRST NOEL

TRADITIONAL ENGLISH CAROL

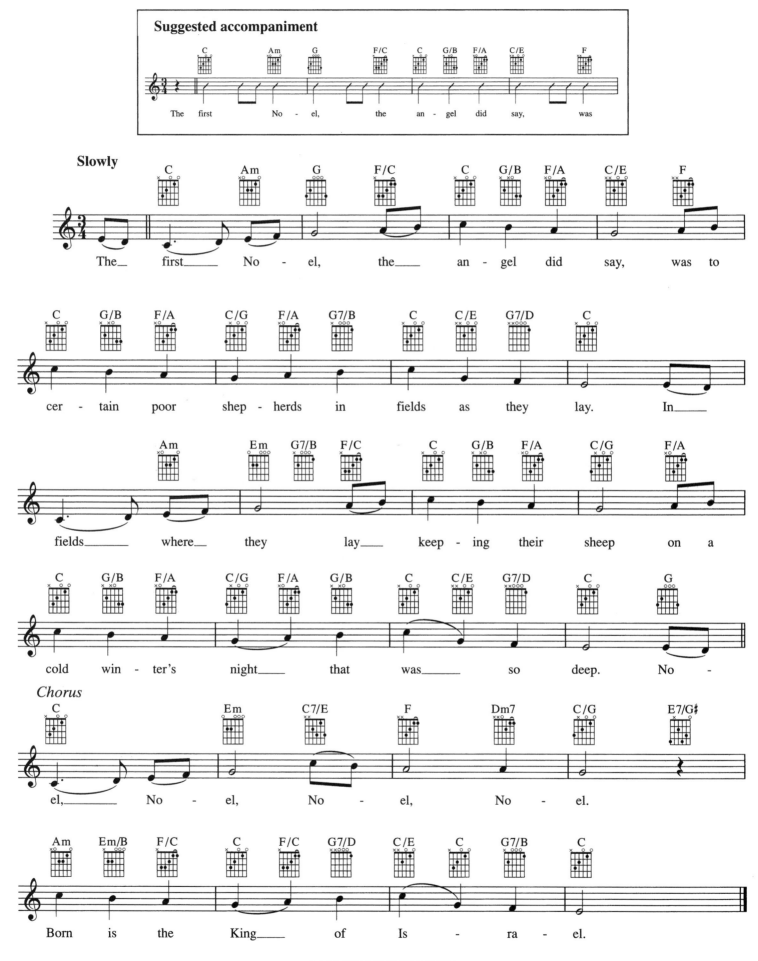

GO TELL IT ON THE MOUNTAIN

TRADITIONAL SPIRITUAL

Verse 3:
While shepherds kept their watching
O'er wand'ring flock by night,
Behold, from out the Heavens
There shown a holy light.
(To Chorus:)

Verse 4:
And lo, when they had seen it,
They all bowed down and prayed.
Then they travelled on together,
To where the Babe was laid.
(To Chorus:)

FROSTY THE SNOWMAN

Words and Music by
STEVE NELSON
and JACK ROLLINS

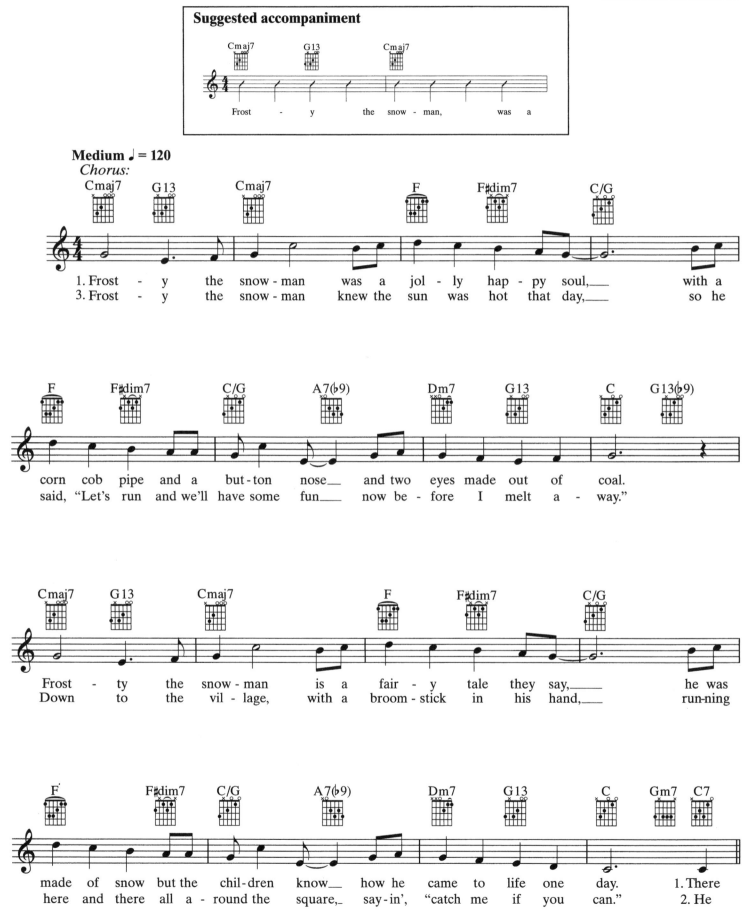

GESÙ BAMBINO

English Lyrics by
FREDERICK H. MARTENS

Music and Italian Lyrics by
PIETRO A. YON

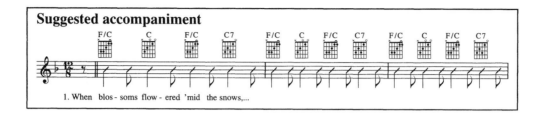

Gesù Bambino (The Infant Jesus) - 2 - 1

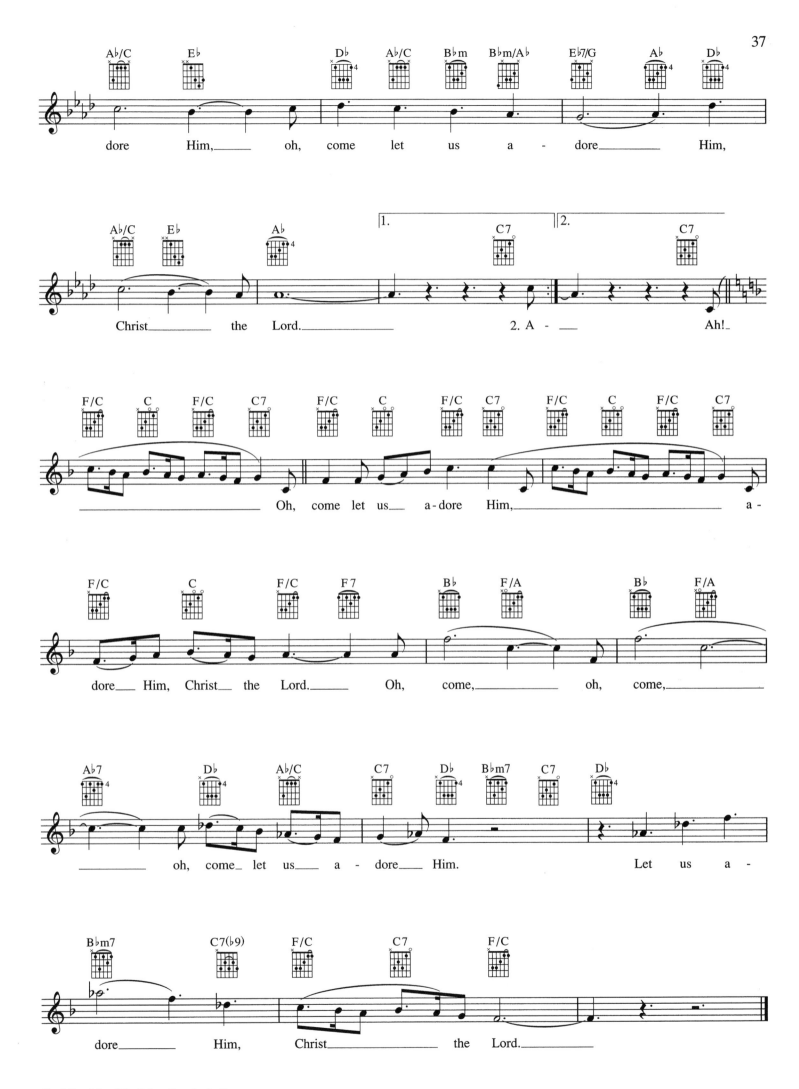

GOD REST YE MERRY, GENTLEMEN

TRADITIONAL ENGLISH CAROL

Suggested accompaniment

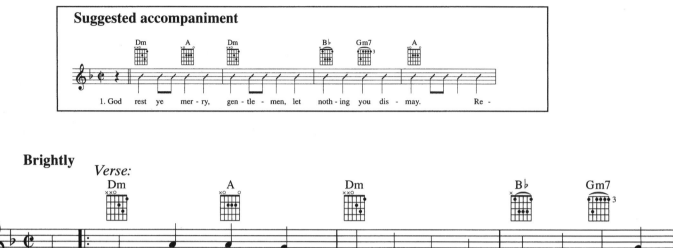

1. God rest ye mer-ry, gen-tle-men, let noth-ing you dis-may. Re-

Brightly *Verse:*

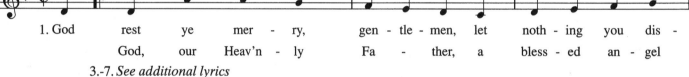

1. God rest ye mer - ry, gen - tle - men, let noth - ing you dis -
God, our Heav'n - ly Fa - ther, a bless - ed an - gel

3.-7. *See additional lyrics*

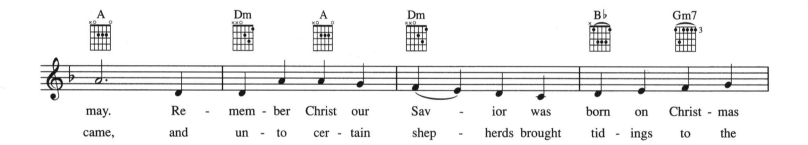

may. Re - mem - ber Christ our Sav - ior was born on Christ - mas
came, and un - to cer - tain shep - herds brought tid - ings to the

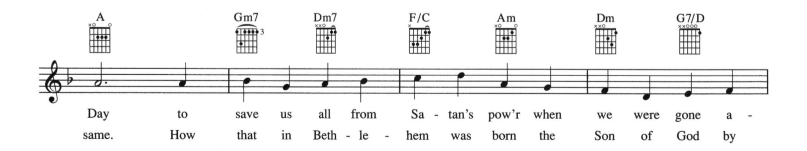

Day to save us all from Sa - tan's pow'r when we were gone a -
same. How that in Beth - le - hem was born the Son of God by

God Rest Ye Merry, Gentlemen - 2 - 1

stray.   Oh,_____ } tid - ings of com - fort and
name.   Oh,_____

joy,   com - fort and joy.   Oh,_____ tid - ings of

com - fort and joy.   { 2. From   joy.
                         { 3. In

Verse 3:
In Bethlehem, in Jewry,
This Blessed Babe was born.
And laid within a manger
Upon this holy morn,
The which his Mother Mary
Did nothing take in scorn.
Oh, tidings...

Verse 4:
"Fear not then," said the angel,
"Let nothing you affright.
This day is born a Savior,
Of a pure Virgin bright,
To free all those who trust in Him
From Satan's power and might."
Oh, tidings...

Verse 5:
The shepherds at those tidings
Rejoiced much in mind,
And left their flocks a-feeding
In tempest, storm, and wind,
And went to Bethlehem straightway,
The Son of God to find.
Oh, tidings...

Verse 6:
And when they came to Bethlehem
Where our dear Savior lay,
They found Him in a manger
Where oxen feed on hay.
His Mother Mary kneeling down,
Unto the Lord did pray.
Oh, tidings...

Verse 7:
Now to the Lord sing praises,
All you within this place.
And with true love and brotherhood
Each other now embrace.
This holy tide of Christmas
All other doth deface.
Oh, tidings...

GOOD CHRISTIAN MEN, REJOICE

Words by
JOHN MASON NEALE

OLD GERMAN SONG

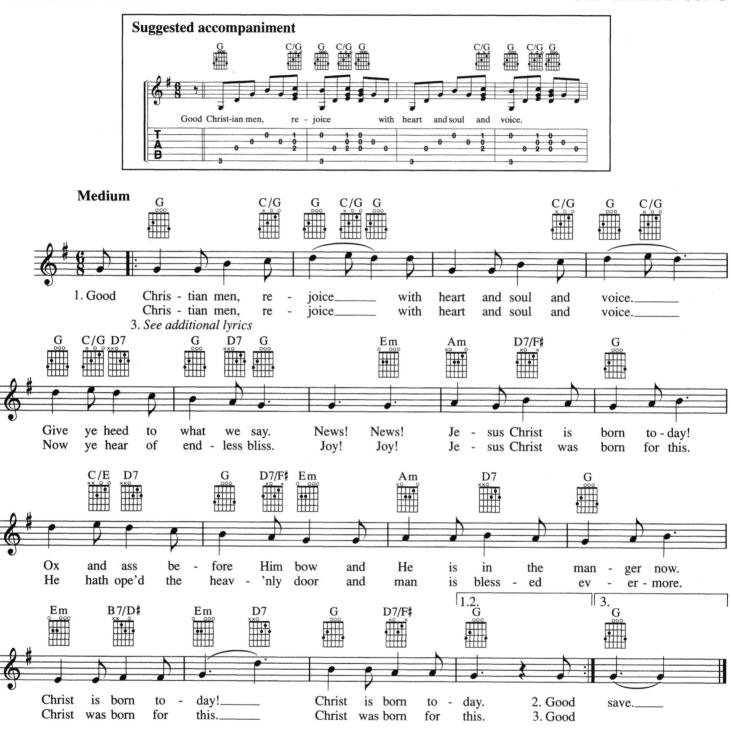

Verse 3:
Good Christian men, rejoice
With heart and soul and voice.
Now ye need not fear the grave:
Peace! Peace!
Jesus Christ was born to save.
Calls you one and calls you all
To gain his everlasting hall.
Christ was born to save;
Christ was born to save.

GOOD KING WENCESLAS

TRADITIONAL ENGLISH CAROL

Medium

Verse:

1. Good King Wen - ces - las looked out on the Feast of Ste - phen.
2. Hith - er, page, and stand by me, if thou know'st it tell - ing.

3.4.5. *See additional lyrics*

When the snow lay 'round a - bout, deep and crisp and e - ven.
Yon - der peas - ant, who is he? Where and what his dwell - ing?

Bright - ly shone the moon that night, though the frost was cru - el. When a poor man
"Sire, he lives a good league hence, un - der - neath the moun - tain, right a - gainst the

came in sight gath - 'ring win - ter fu - el. ing.
for - est fence by St. Ag - nes foun - tain.

Verse 3:
"Bring me flesh and bring me wine, bring me pine logs hither.
Thou and I will see him dine, when we bear him thither."
Page and monarch forth they went, forth they went together,
Through the rude wind's wild lament and the bitter weather.

Verse 4:
"Sire, the night is darker now, and the wind blows stronger.
Fails my heart, I know not how, I can go no longer."
"Mark my footsteps, my good page, tread thou in them boldly.
Thou shalt find the winter's rage freeze thy blood less coldly."

Verse 5:
In his master's steps he trod, where the snow lay dinted.
Heat was in the very sod which the Saint had printed.
Therefore, Christian men, be sure, wealth or rank possessing;
Ye who will now bless the poor shall yourselves find blessing.

A GREAT AND MIGHTY WONDER

TRADITIONAL GERMAN SONG

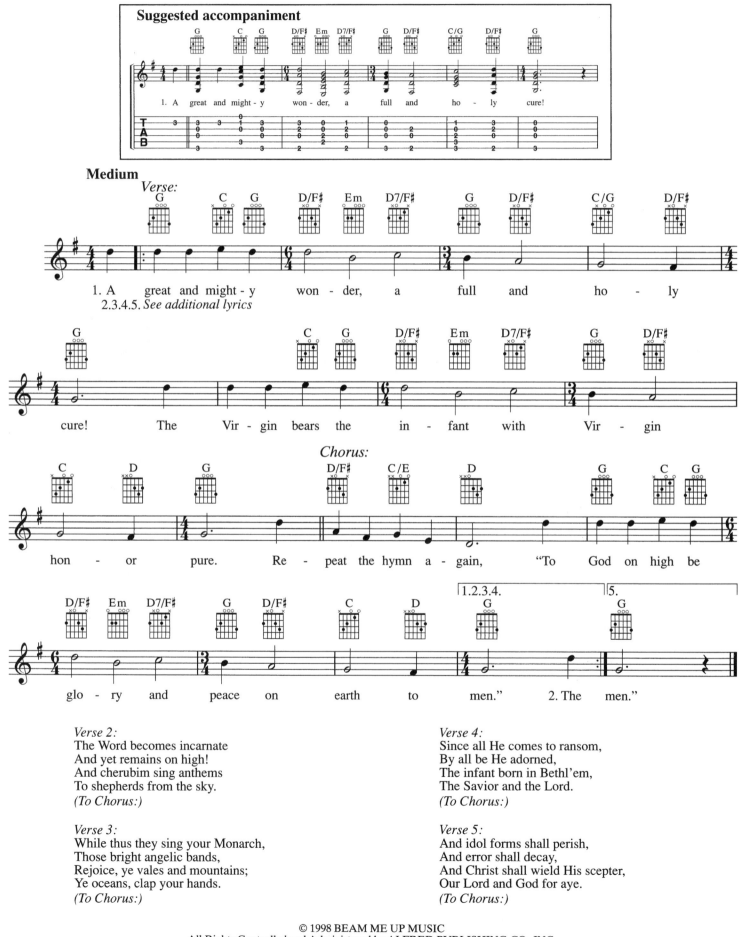

Verse 2:
The Word becomes incarnate
And yet remains on high!
And cherubim sing anthems
To shepherds from the sky.
(To Chorus:)

Verse 3:
While thus they sing your Monarch,
Those bright angelic bands,
Rejoice, ye vales and mountains;
Ye oceans, clap your hands.
(To Chorus:)

Verse 4:
Since all He comes to ransom,
By all be He adorned,
The infant born in Bethl'em,
The Savior and the Lord.
(To Chorus:)

Verse 5:
And idol forms shall perish,
And error shall decay,
And Christ shall wield His scepter,
Our Lord and God for aye.
(To Chorus:)

GROWN-UP CHRISTMAS LIST

Words and Music by
DAVID FOSTER and LINDA THOMPSON JENNER

Grown-up Christmas List - 3 - 1

HARK! THE HERALD ANGELS SING

Words by
CHAS. WESLEY

Music by
FELIX MENDELSSOHN

Suggested accompaniment

1. Hark! The her - ald an - gels sing, "Glo - ry to the new - born King!"

Moderate ballad

1. Hark! The her - ald an - gels sing,___ "Glo - ry to the new - born King!
2. Christ, by high - est heav'n a - dored,___ Christ, the ev - er - last - ing Lord.
3. *See additional lyrics*

Peace on earth and mer - cy mild;___ God and sin - ners rec - on - ciled."
Late in time be - hold Him come,___ off - spring of the Vir - gin's womb.

Joy - ful, all ye na - tions rise,___ join the tri - umph of the skies.___
Veiled in flesh the God - head see,___ hail th'in - car - nate De - i - ty.___

With an - gel - ic host pro - claim, "Christ is___ born in Beth - le - hem."
Pleased as man with men ap - pear, Je - sus,___ our Im - man - uel here.

Hark! The her - ald an - gels sing, "Glo - ry___ to the new - born King!"
Hark! The her - ald an - gels sing, "Glo - ry___ to the new - born King!"

Verse 3:
Hail the heav'n born Prince of Peace,
Hail the Son of righteousness!
Light and life to all He brings,
Ris'n with healing in His wings.
Mild, He lays His glory by,
Born that man no more may die,
Born to raise the sons of earth,
Born to give them second birth.
Hark! The herald angels sing,
"Glory to the newborn King!"

HERE WE COME A-WASSAILING

OLD ENGLISH

Verse 2:
We are not daily beggars
That beg from door to door.
But we are neighbors' children
Whom you have seen before.
(To Chorus:)

Verse 3:
We have got a little purse
Of stretching leather skin,
We want a little of your money
To line it well within.
(To Chorus:)

Verse 4:
Bring us out a table,
And spread it with a cloth;
Bring us out a moldy cheese,
And some of your Christmas loaf.
(To Chorus:)

Verse 5:
God bless the master of this house,
Likewise the mistress too,
And all the little children
That 'round the table go.
(To Chorus:)

HAVE YOURSELF A
MERRY LITTLE CHRISTMAS

Words and Music by
HUGH MARTIN and RALPH BLANE

Have Yourself a Merry Little Christmas - 2 - 1

THE HOLLY AND THE IVY

TRADITIONAL ENGLISH

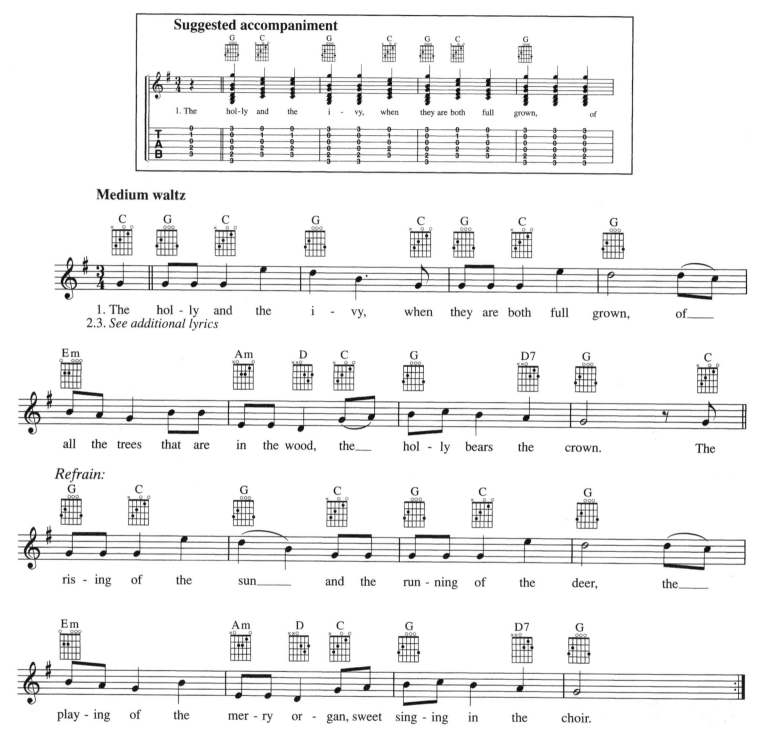

1. The hol-ly and the i-vy, when they are both full grown, of___
2.3. *See additional lyrics*

all the trees that are in the wood, the___ hol-ly bears the crown. The

Refrain:

ris-ing of the sun___ and the run-ning of the deer, the___

play-ing of the mer-ry or-gan, sweet sing-ing in the choir.

Verse 2:
The holly bears a blossom
As white as lily flow'r,
And Mary bore sweet Jesus Christ
To be our sweet Savior.
(To Refrain:)

Verse 3:
The holly bears a berry
As red as any blood,
And Mary bore sweet Jesus Christ
To do poor sinners good.
(To Refrain:)

HOLY NIGHT, PEACEFUL NIGHT

Words and Music by
SIR JOSEPH BARNBY

(There's No Place Like)
HOME FOR THE HOLIDAYS

Words by
AL STILLMAN

Music by
ROBERT ALLEN

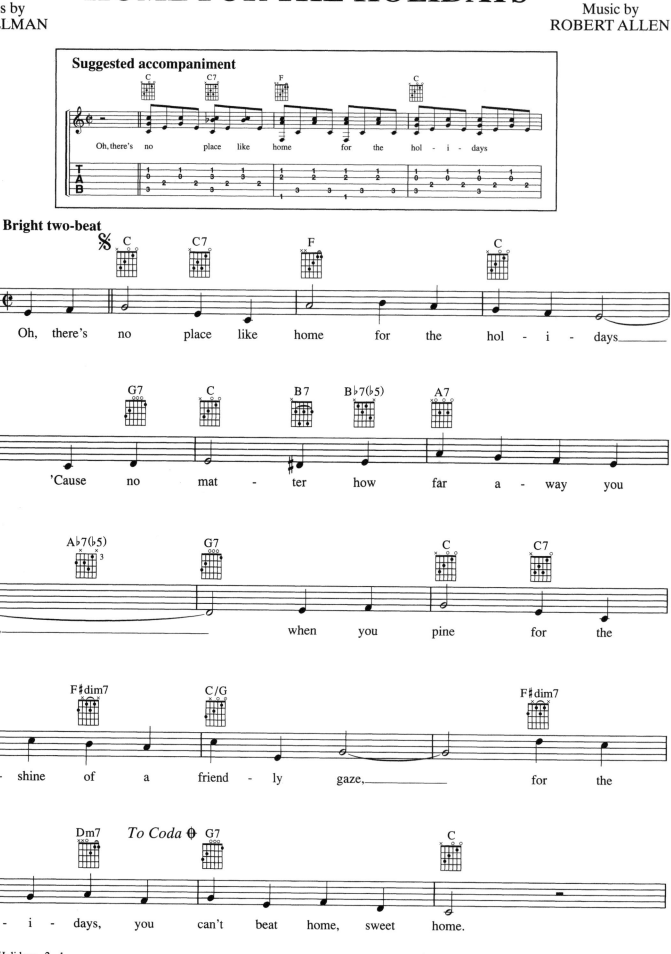

Home for the Holidays - 2 - 1

I met a man who lives in Ten - nes - see and
he was head - in' for Penn - syl - va - nia and some
home - made pump - kin pie. From Penn - syl -
va - nia, folks are trav - 'lin' down to Dix - ie's sun - ny
shore; from At - lan - tic to Pa - cif - ic, gee, the

D.S. 𝄋 al Coda

traf - fic is ter - rif - ic. Oh, there's

Coda

can't beat home, sweet home.

HUSH, MY BABE, LIE STILL AND SLUMBER

ISAAC WATTS

TRADITIONAL AMERICAN

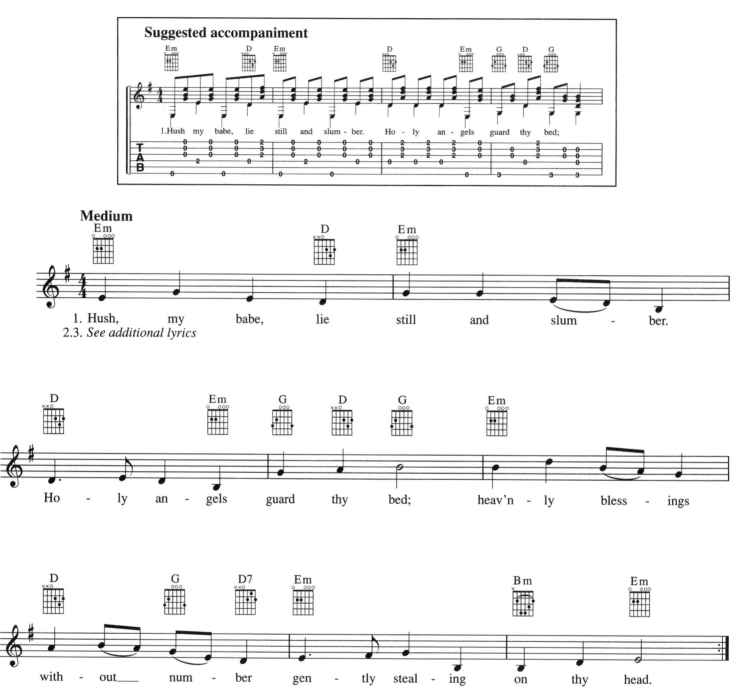

Verse 2:
How much better art thou attended
Than the Son of God could be;
When from Heaven He descended
And became a child like thee.

Verse 3:
Soft and easy is thy cradle,
Coarse and hard the Savior lay
When His birthplace was a stable,
And His softest bed was hay.

I HEARD THE BELLS ON CHRISTMAS DAY

Words by
HENRY WADSWORTH LONGFELLOW

Music by
HENRY BISHOP

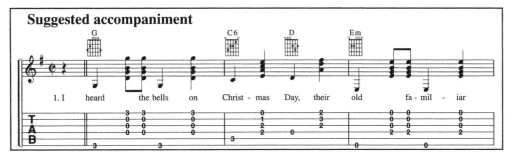

Suggested accompaniment

Medium

1. I heard the bells on Christ-mas Day, their old fa-mil - iar
   in de - spair, I bowed my head, "there is no peace on

car - ols play. And wild and sweet the words re - peat, of peace on earth, good
earth," I said. "For hate is strong and mocks the song of peace on earth, good

will to men. I thought, as now this day had come, the bel - fries of all
will to men." Then pealed the bells more loud and deep, "God is not dead, nor

Chris - ten - dom had rung so long the un - bro - ken song of
doth He sleep." "The wrong shall fail, the right pre - vail, with

peace on earth, good will to men. 2. And will to men."
peace on earth, good

I SAW THREE SHIPS

TRADITIONAL ENGLISH CAROL

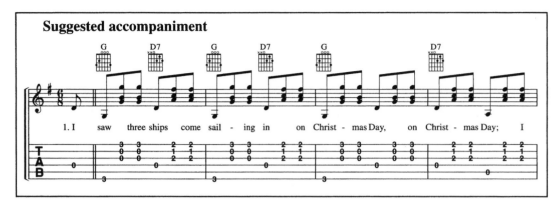

Suggested accompaniment

1. I saw three ships come sail - ing in on Christ - mas Day, on Christ - mas Day; I

Moderately

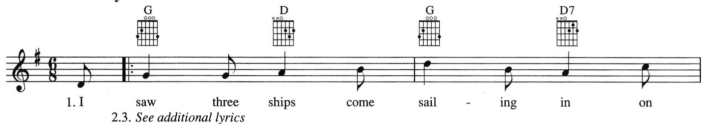

1. I saw three ships come sail - ing in on
2.3. *See additional lyrics*

Christ - mas Day, on Christ - mas Day; I saw three ships come

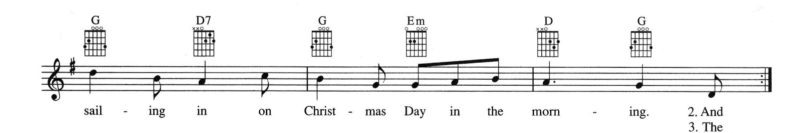

sail - ing in on Christ - mas Day in the morn - ing.
2. And
3. The

Verse 2:
And what was in those ships all three
On Christmas Day, on Christmas Day;
And what was in those ships all three
On Christmas Day in the morning.

Verse 3:
The Virgin Mary and Christ were there
On Christmas Day, on Christmas Day;
The Virgin Mary and Christ were there
On Christmas Day in the morning.

I'LL BE HOME FOR CHRISTMAS

Words by
KIM GANNON

Music by
WALTER KENT

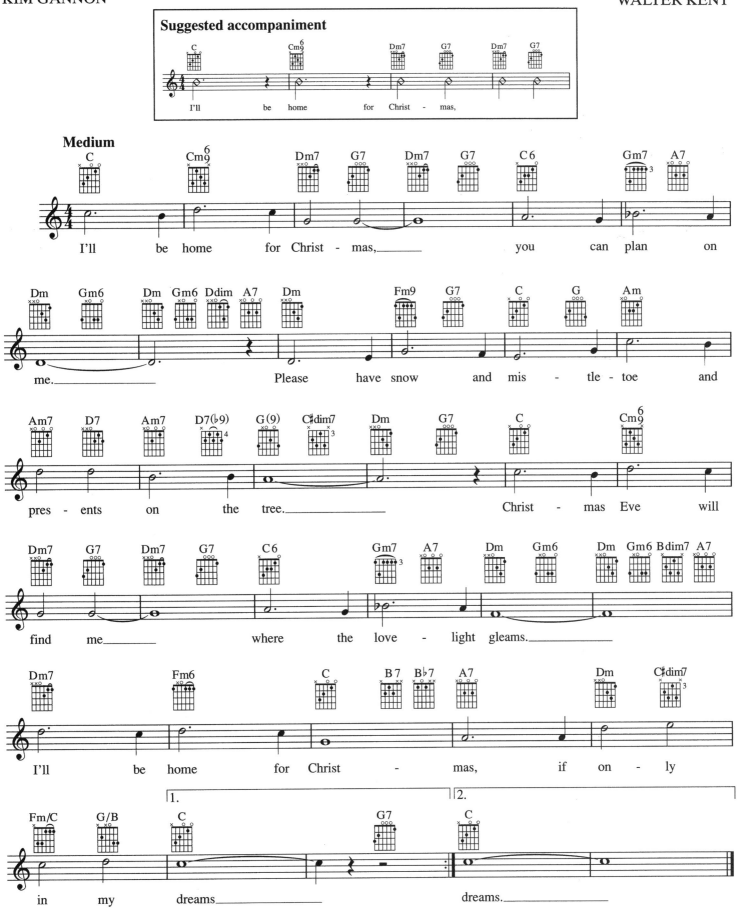

IN A CHRISTMAS MOOD

Lyrics by
JUDY SPENCER

Music by
EARL ROSE

IT CAME UPON THE MIDNIGHT CLEAR

Words by
RICHARD S. WILLIS

Music by
EDMUND H. SEARS

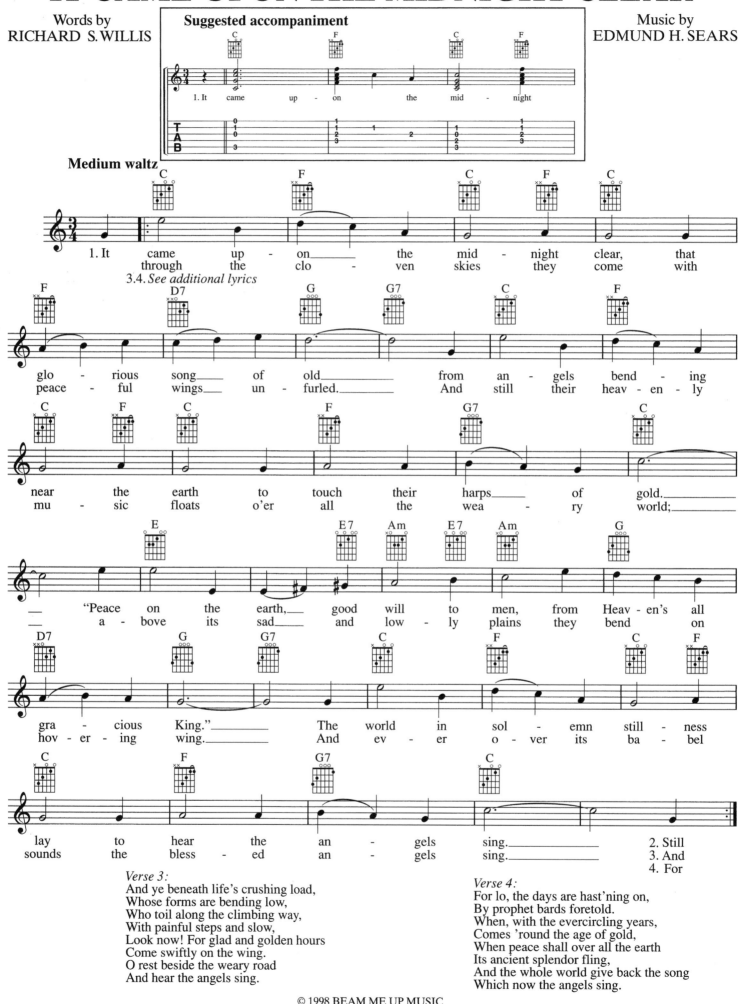

Medium waltz

1. It came up-on the mid-night clear, that
through the clo-ven skies they come with
3.4. See additional lyrics

glo-rious song of old from an-gels bend-ing
peace-ful wings un-furled. And still their heav-en-ly

near the earth to touch their harps of gold.
mu-sic floats o'er all the wea-ry world;

"Peace on the earth, good will to men, from Heav-en's all
a-bove its sad and low-ly plains they bend on

gra-cious King." The world in sol-emn still-ness
hov-er-ing wing. And ev-er o-ver its ba-bel

lay to hear the an-gels sing. 2. Still
sounds the bless-ed an-gels sing. 3. And
4. For

Verse 3:
And ye beneath life's crushing load,
Whose forms are bending low,
Who toil along the climbing way,
With painful steps and slow,
Look now! For glad and golden hours
Come swiftly on the wing.
O rest beside the weary road
And hear the angels sing.

Verse 4:
For lo, the days are hast'ning on,
By prophet bards foretold.
When, with the evercircling years,
Comes 'round the age of gold,
When peace shall over all the earth
Its ancient splendor fling,
And the whole world give back the song
Which now the angels sing.

JINGLE BELLS

Words and Music by
J. PIERPONT

IT MUST HAVE BEEN THE MISTLETOE

Words and Music by
JUSTIN WILDE and DOUG KONECKY

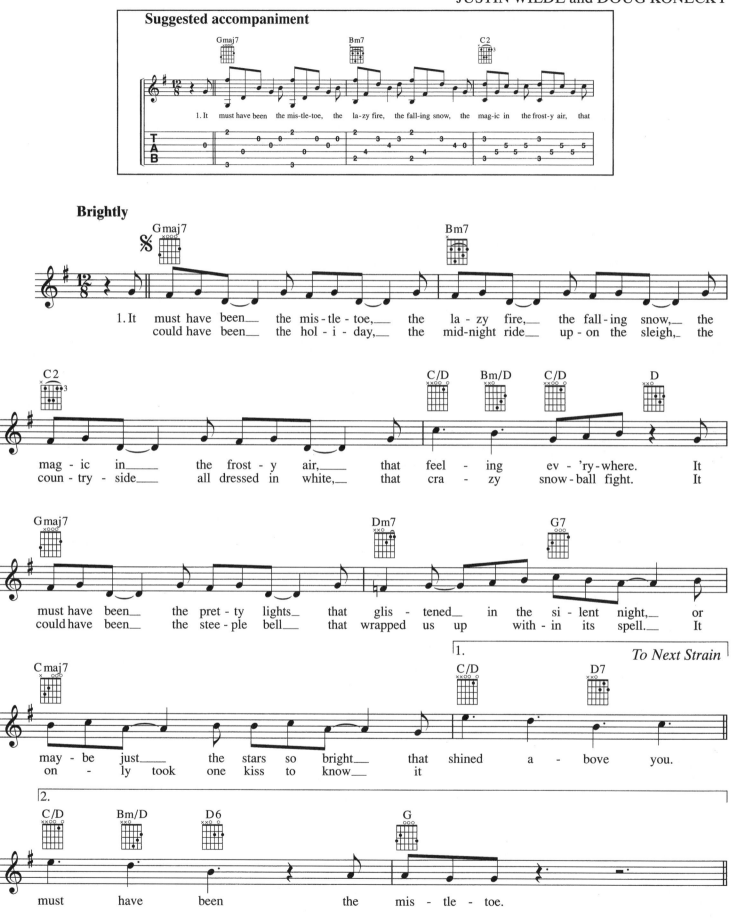

It Must Have Been the Mistletoe - 2 - 1

Chorus:

Our first Christ - mas; more than___ we'd been dream - ing of.___

_____ Old Saint Nich - 'las { had his fin - gers crossed that
{ must have known that kiss would

1. we would fall in love.___

D.S. 𝄋 2. It lead to all of this._____ It

must have been___ the mis-tle-toe,___ the la-zy fire,___ the fall-ing snow,___ the mag-ic in___ the frost-y air___ that

made me love you. On Christ-mas Eve___ a wish came true,___ that night I___ fell in love with you.___ It

on - ly took___ one kiss to know___ it must have been the mis-tle-toe. It

must have been the mis-tle-toe. It must have been the mis-tle-toe.

IT'S CHRISTMAS IN NEW YORK

Words and Music by
BILLY BUTT

It's Christmas in New York - 2 - 1

Verse 3:
Stockings are filling, champagne is chilling.
It's all so thrilling, it's Christmas in New York.
Log fires are burning,
Santa's returning, filling each yearning,
It's Christmas in New York.
(To Verse 4:)

IT'S THE MOST
WONDERFUL TIME OF THE YEAR

By
EDDIE POLA and
GEORGE WYLE

It's the Most Wonderful Time of the Year - 2 - 1

JINGLE BELL ROCK

Words and Music by
JOE BEAL and JIM BOOTHE

JOLLY OLD SAINT NICHOLAS

TRADITIONAL

JOY TO THE WORLD

Words by
ISAAC WATTS

Music by
GEORGE F. HANDEL

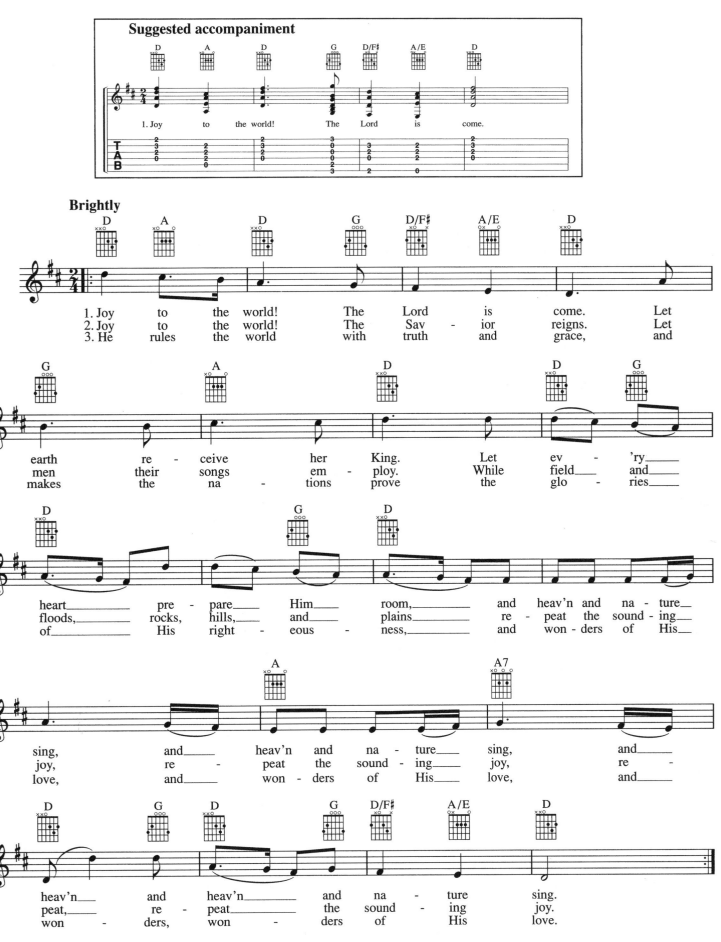

LET IT SNOW! LET IT SNOW! LET IT SNOW!

Words by SAMMY CAHN
Music by JULE STYNE

Moderate swing feel

Verse 2:
It doesn't show signs of stopping,
And I brought some corn for popping.
The lights are turned way down low.
Let it snow, let it snow, let it snow!
(To Bridge:)

Verse 3:
The fire is slowly dying,
And, my dear, we're still goodbyeing,
But as long as you love me so,
Let it snow, let it snow, let it snow!

MARY HAD A BABY

TRADITIONAL

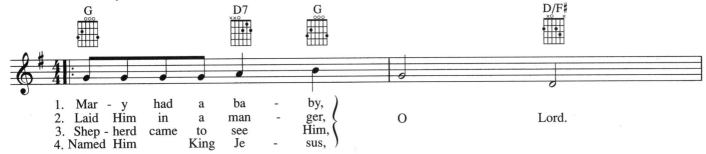

Moderately

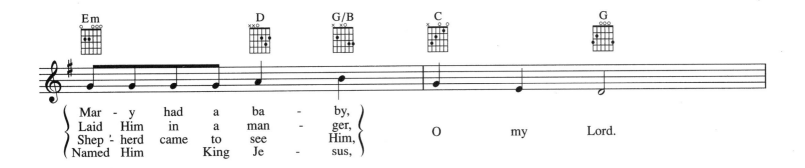

1. Mar - y had a ba - by,
2. Laid Him in a man - ger,
3. Shep - herd came to see Him,
4. Named Him King Je - sus,

O Lord.

Mar - y had a ba - by,
Laid Him in a man - ger,
Shep - herd came to see Him,
Named Him King Je - sus,

O my Lord.

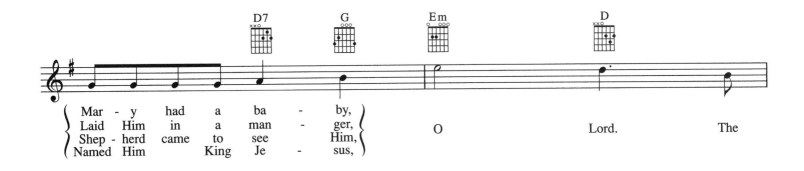

Mar - y had a ba - by,
Laid Him in a man - ger,
Shep - herd came to see Him,
Named Him King Je - sus,

O Lord. The

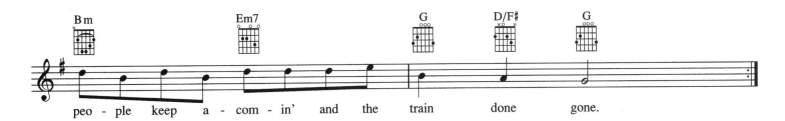

peo - ple keep a - com - in' and the train done gone.

LET'S HAVE AN OLD-FASHIONED CHRISTMAS

Words by
HAROLD ADAMSON

Music by
JIMMY McHUGH

Let's Have an Old-Fashioned Christmas - 2 - 1

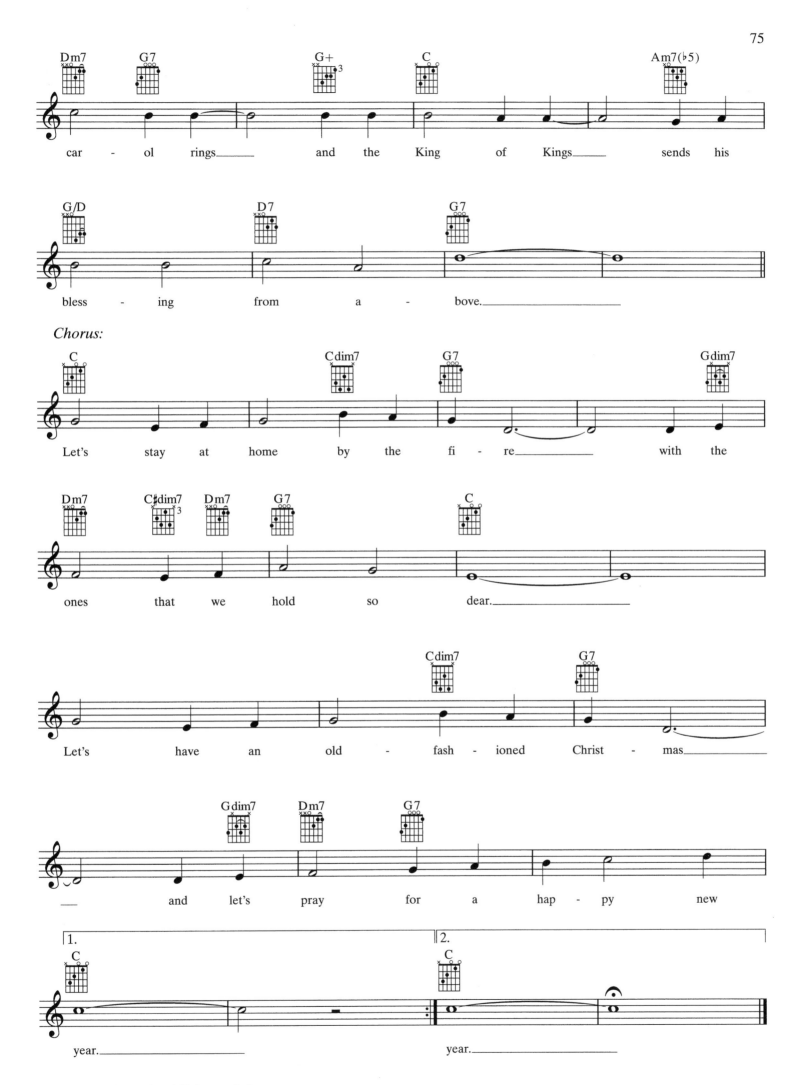

Let's Have an Old-Fashioned Christmas - 2 - 2

THE LITTLE DRUMMER BOY

Words and Music by
KATHERINE DAVIS, HENRY ONORATI
and HARRY SIMEONE

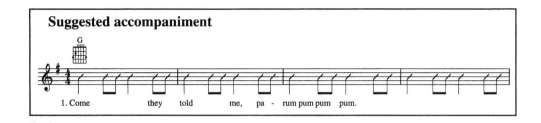

Suggested accompaniment

1. Come they told me, pa - rum pum pum pum.

Moderately

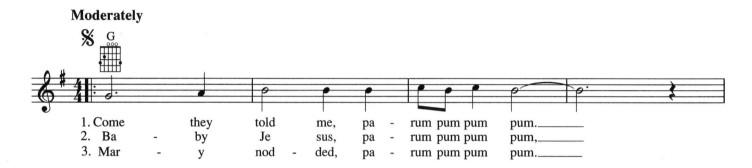

1. Come they told me, pa - rum pum pum pum._____
2. Ba - by Je - sus, pa - rum pum pum pum,_____
3. Mar - y nod - ded, pa - rum pum pum pum._____

Our new born King to see, pa - rum pum pum pum._____
I am a poor boy too, pa - rum pum pum pum._____
The ox and lamb kept time, pa - rum pum pum pum._____

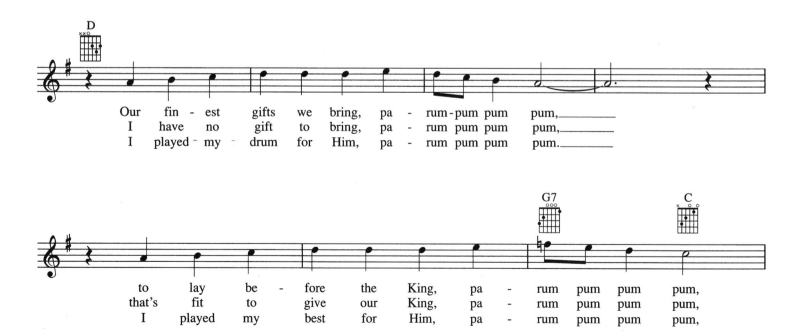

Our fin - est gifts we bring, pa - rum-pum pum pum,_____
I have no gift to bring, pa - rum pum pum pum,_____
I played my drum for Him, pa - rum pum pum pum._____

to lay be - fore the King, pa - rum pum pum pum,
that's fit to give our King, pa - rum pum pum pum,
I played my best for Him, pa - rum pum pum pum,

The Little Drummer Boy - 2 - 1

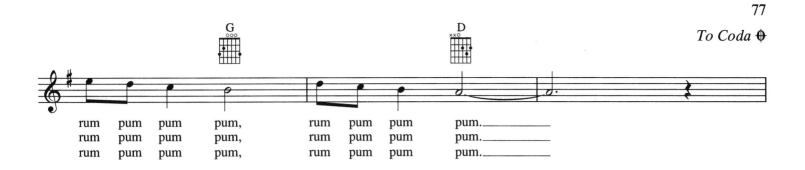

To Coda ⊕

rum pum pum pum,   rum pum pum pum._____
rum pum pum pum,   rum pum pum pum._____
rum pum pum pum,   rum pum pum pum._____

So   to   hon - or   Him,   pa - rum pum pum   pum,_____
Shall   I   play   for You,   pa - rum pum pum   pum,_____

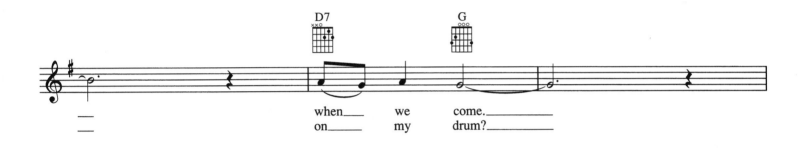

_   when___ we   come._____
_   on_____ my   drum?_____

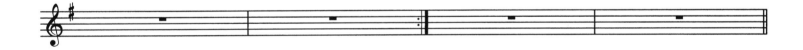

1.   2.   *D.S.* 𝄋 *al Coda*

⊕
Coda

Then   He   smiled at   me,   pa -

rum pum pum   pum,_____   me and my   drum._____

MARCH OF THE TOYS

Music by
VICTOR HERBERT

Bright march tempo

March of the Toys - 2 - 1

D.S. 𝄋 al Coda

Coda

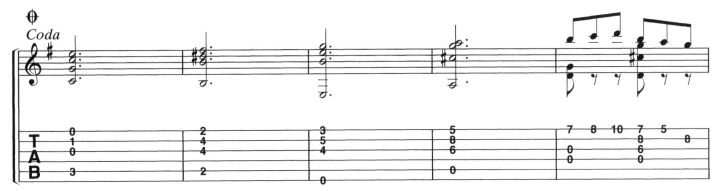

March of the Toys - 2 - 2

NESTOR, THE LONG-EARED CHRISTMAS DONKEY

Words and Music by
GENE AUTRY, DON PFRIMMER
and DAVE BURGESS

Nestor, the Long-Eared Christmas Donkey - 2 - 1

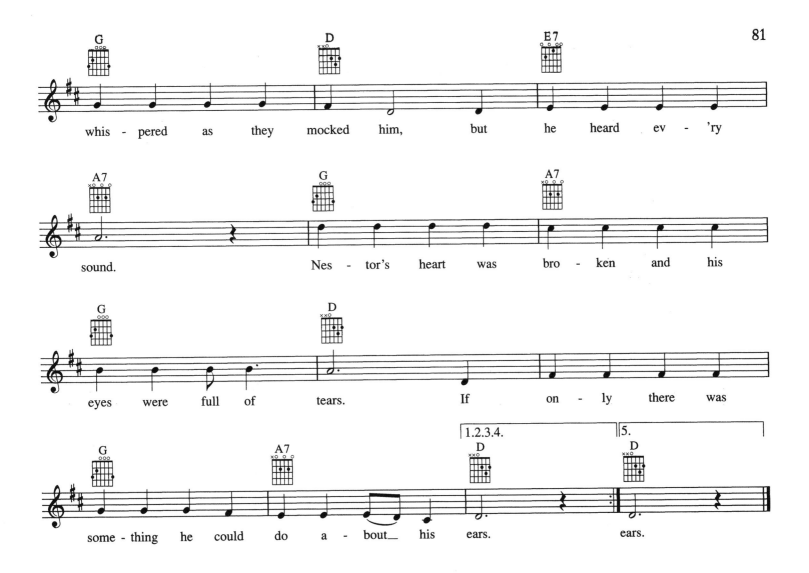

whis - pered as they mocked him, but he heard ev - 'ry

sound. Nes - tor's heart was bro - ken and his

eyes were full of tears. If on - ly there was

1.2.3.4.   5.

some - thing he could do a - bout_ his ears. ears.

Verse 3:
They traveled through the desert, but hadn't gone too far,
When winter clouds no longer let them see their guiding star.
But Nestor had a secret, only he could hear the sound,
As the angels gave directions to the ears that dragged the ground.
(To Chorus:)

Verse 4:
And so it was that Nestor found the manger where they stayed,
Where kings and wisemen bowed before a baby where he laid.
Mary bore our Savior and Nestor brought them there,
A gift of love from God above for all the world to share.
(To Chorus:)

Verse 5:
Though, Rudolph, I just love you, I know you'd want it said,
Nestor's ears are lovely as a reindeer's nose is red.
So, children, if you're happy when you trim your Christmas trees,
You might thank a little donkey whose ears hang to his knees.

Chorus 5:
"Look at little Nestor, he's got ears that drag the ground,"
They shouted as they praised him,
And his friends all gathered 'round.
Nestor's heart grew happy and his eyes held no more tears,
Now all the world knows Nestor for his laughter and his ears.

NOEL! NOEL!

TRADITIONAL

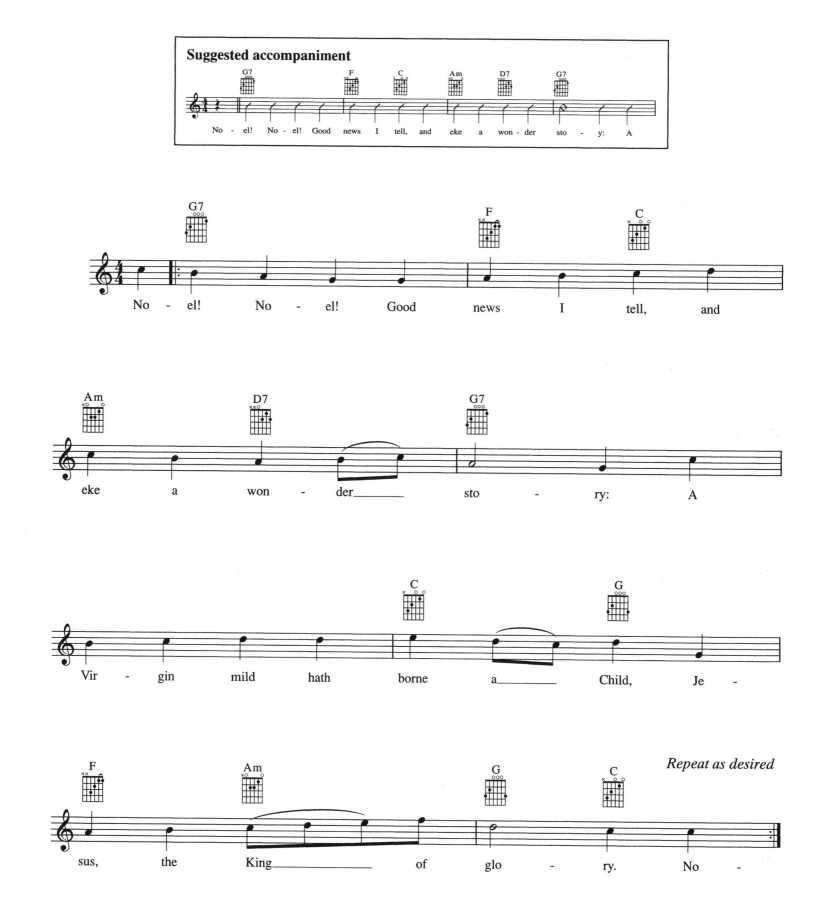

O CHRISTMAS TREE
(O Tannenbaum)

OLD GERMAN CAROL

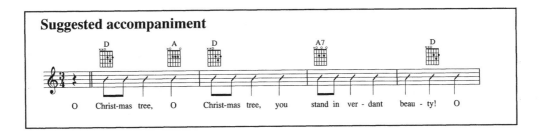

NUTTIN' FOR CHRISTMAS

Words and Music by
SID TEPPER and ROY C. BENNETT

Nuttin' for Christmas - 2 - 1

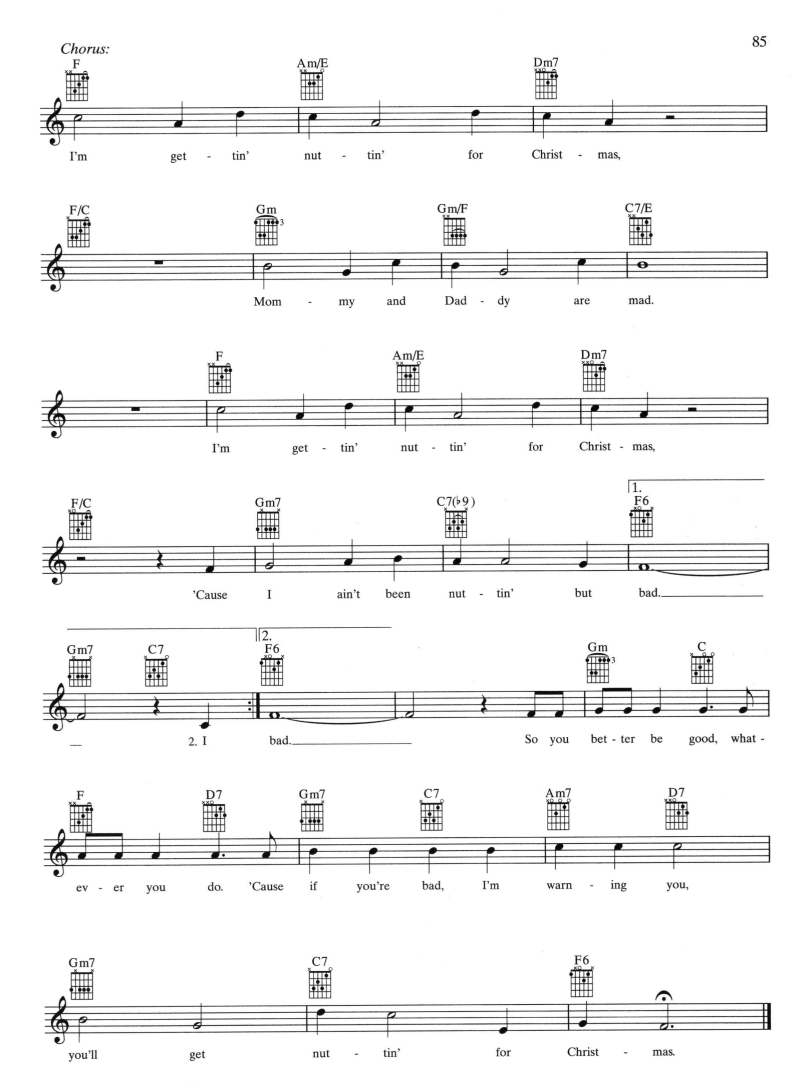

O COME, ALL YE FAITHFUL
(Adeste Fideles)

English Words by
FREDERICK OAKELEY
Latin Words Attributed to
JOHN FRANCIS WADE

Music by
JOHN READING

Verse 3:
Yea, Lord, we greet Thee,
Born this happy morning.
Jesus, to Thee be glory giv'n.
Word of the Father,
Now in flesh appearing.
O come, let us adore him,...

O COME, LITTLE CHILDREN

Words and Music by
CHRISTOPH VAN SCHMIDT
and J.A.P. SCHULTZ

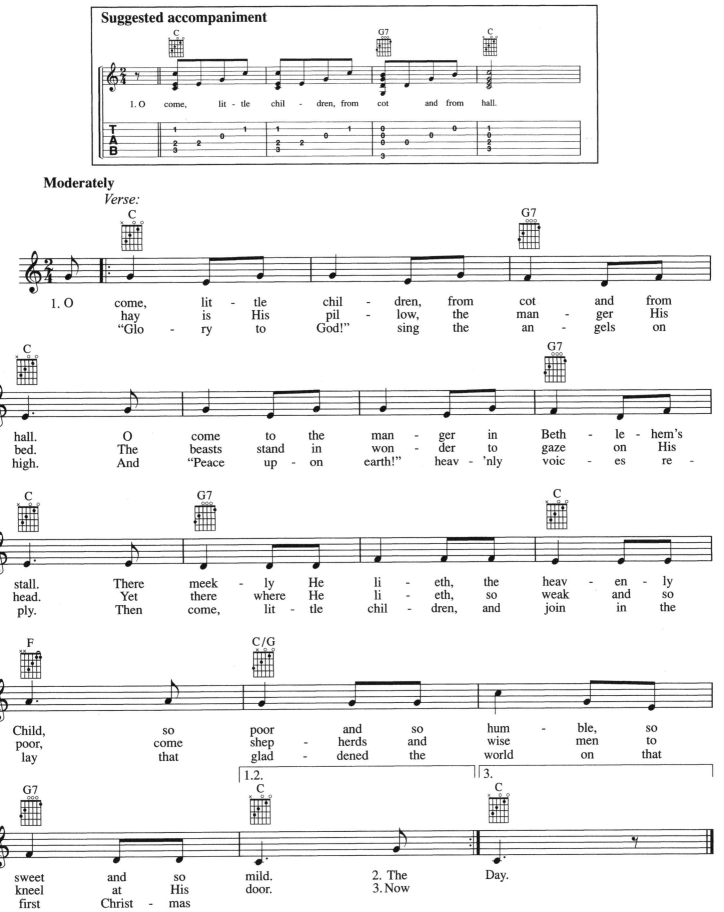

O COME, O COME EMMANUEL

TRADITIONAL

Verse 3:
O come, Thou Day-Spring, come and cheer
Our spirits by Thine advent here;
Disperse the gloomy clouds of night,
And death's dark shadows put to fight.
(To Chorus:)

Verse 4:
O come, Thou Key of David, come,
And open wide our heav'nly home;
Make safe the way that leads on high,
And close the path to misery.
(To Chorus:)

Verse 5:
O come, O come, Thou Lord of might,
Who to Thy tribes, on Sinai's height,
In ancient times did'st give the law,
In cloud and majesty and awe.
(To Chorus:)

O HOLY NIGHT

Words by
JOHN SULLIVAN DWIGHT

Music by
ADOLPHE CHARLES ADAM

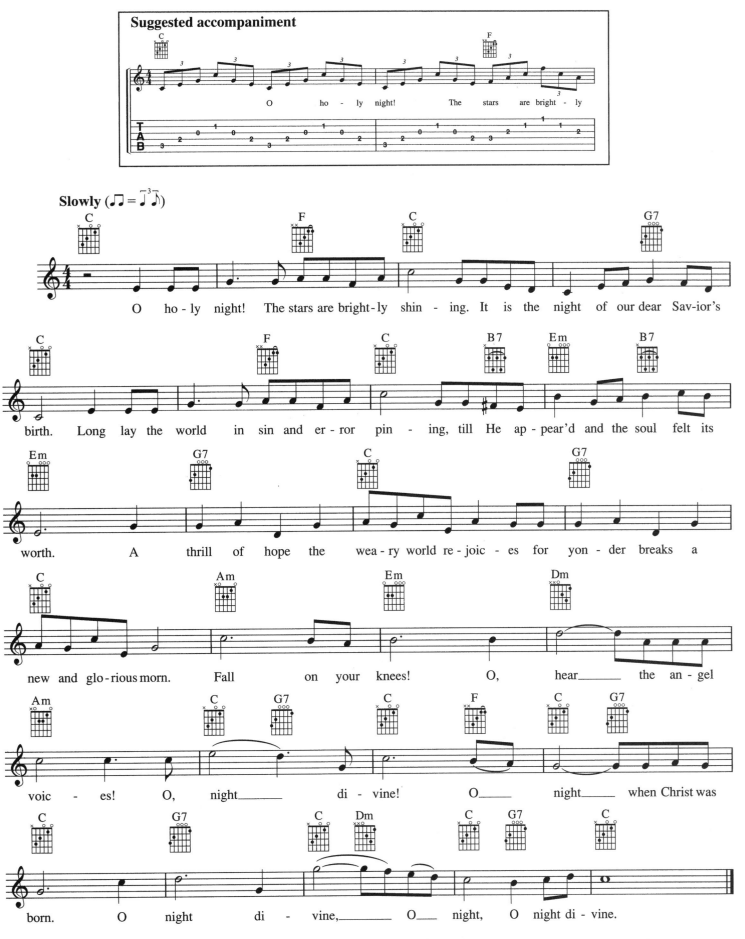

O LITTLE TOWN OF BETHLEHEM

Words by
PHILLIPS BROOKS

Music by
LEWIS H. REDNER

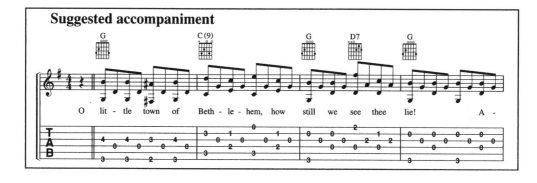

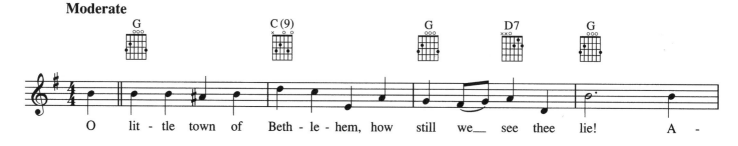

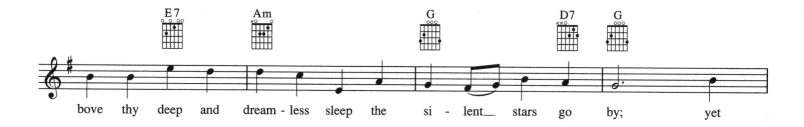

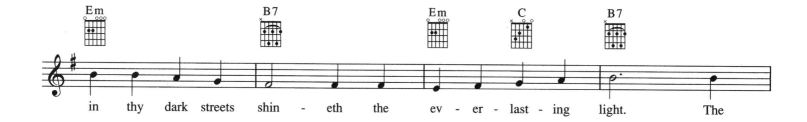

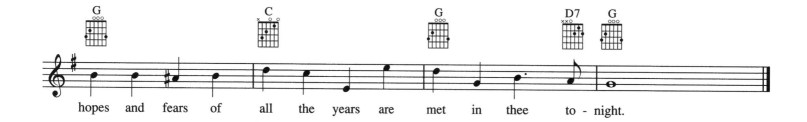

ON CHRISTMAS NIGHT ALL CHRISTIANS SING

TRADITIONAL

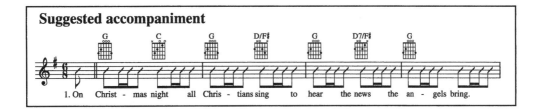

Verse 2:
Then why should men on earth be so sad,
Since our Redeemer made us glad?
Then why should men on earth be so sad,
When from our sin He set us free?
All for to gain our liberty.

Verse 3:
When sin departs before His grace,
Then life and health come in its place.
When sin departs before His grace,
Then life and health come in its place.
Angels and men with joy may sing,
All for to see the newborn King.

ONCE IN ROYAL DAVID'S CITY

Words by
MRS. C. F. ALEXANDER

Music by
H. J. GAUNTLETT

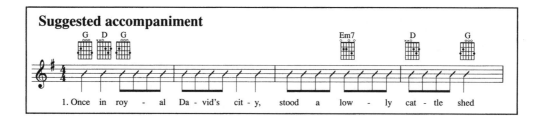

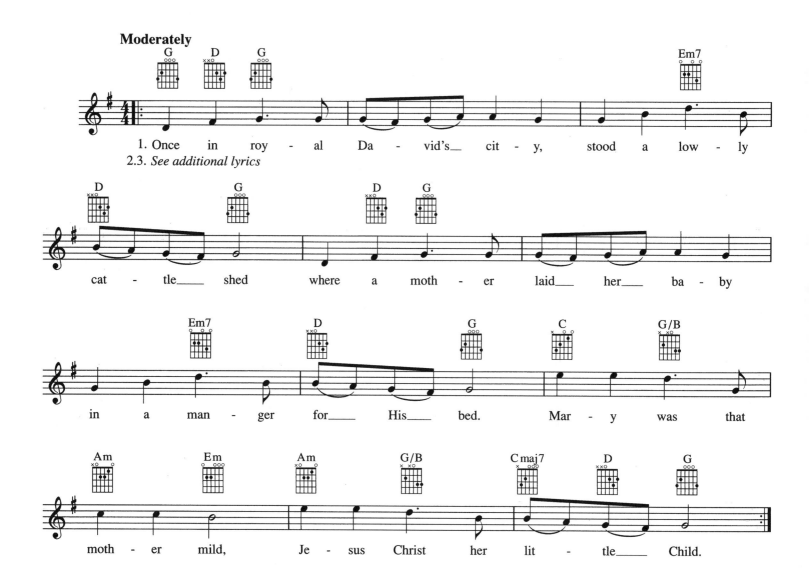

Verse 2:
He came down to Earth from Heaven,
Who is God and Lord of all.
And His shelter was a stable,
And His cradle was a stall.
With the poor and mean and lowly,
Lived on earth our Savior holy.

Verse 3:
And our eyes at last shall see Him,
Through His own redeeming love.
For that Child so dear and gentle
Is our Lord in Heaven above.
And He leads His children on
To the place where He is gone.

PATAPAN

BURGUNDIAN CAROL

Verse 2:
When the men of olden days
Gave the King of Kings their praise,
They had pipes on which to play,
Turelurelu, patapatapan.
They had drums on which to play,
Full of joy, on Christmas Day.

Verse 3:
God and man this day become
Joined as one with flute and drum.
Let the happy time play on,
Turelurelu, patapatapan.
Flute and drum together play,
As we sing on Christmas Day.

SANTA CLAUS IS COMIN' TO TOWN

Words by
HAVEN GILLESPIE

Music by
J. FRED COOTS

SILENT NIGHT

Words and Music by
JOSEPH MOHR and
FRANZ GRUBER

SIMPLE GIFTS

OLD QUAKER MELODY

SLEIGH RIDE

Words by
MITCHELL PARISH

Music by
LEROY ANDERSON

STAND BENEATH THE MISTLETOE

By
LOUIS HOLLINGSWORTH

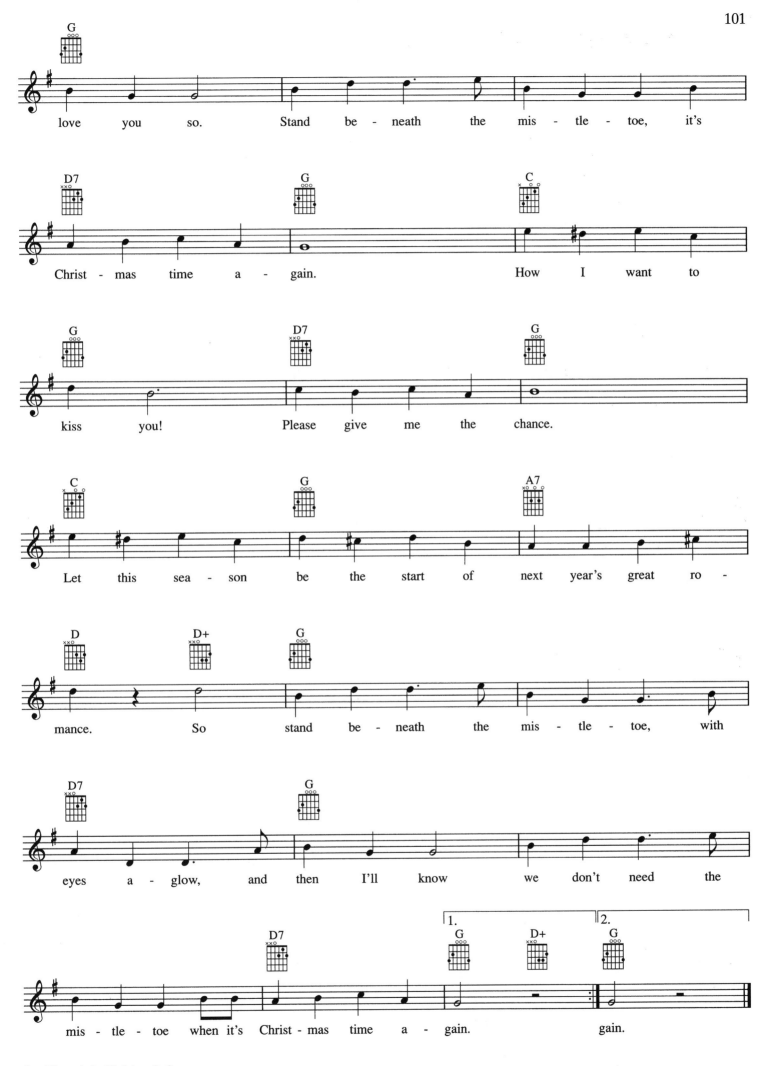

STAR OF THE EAST

Words by
GEORGE COOPER

Music by
AMANDA KENNEDY

THERE IS NO CHRISTMAS
LIKE A HOME CHRISTMAS

Words by
CARL SIGMAN

Music by
MICKEY J. ADDY

SUZY SNOWFLAKE

Words and Music by
SID TEPPER and ROY BRODSKY

Moderately

Refrain:

Here comes Su-zy Snow-flake, dressed in a snow white gown, tap, tap, tap-pin' at your win-dow pane to tell you she's in town. Here comes Su-zy Snow-flake, soon you will hear her say: Come out ev-'ry-one and play with me, I have-n't long to

Suzy Snowflake - 2 - 1

stay.   If you wan - na make   a   snow - man

I'll   help you make   one,   one, two, three.   If you wan - na take   a

sleigh - ride,   the ride's   on   me.

Here   comes   Su - zy   Snow - flake,   look   at her tumb - lin'

down,   bring - ing   joy   to   ev - 'ry   girl   and   boy.

1.
Su - zy's   come   to   town.   Su -   zy's

2.

G7   C   F   C

come   to   town._____

THE TWELVE DAYS OF CHRISTMAS

TRADITIONAL

The Twelve Days of Christmas - 2 - 1

UKRAINIAN CAROL
(Carol of the Bells)

TRADITIONAL

Ukrainian Carol - 2 - 1

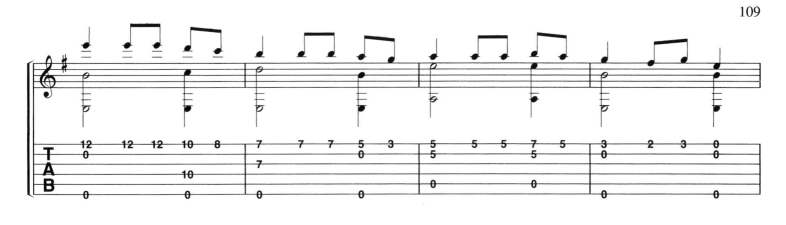

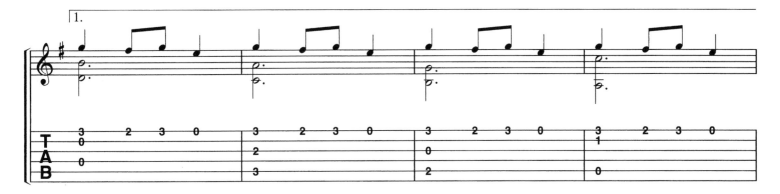

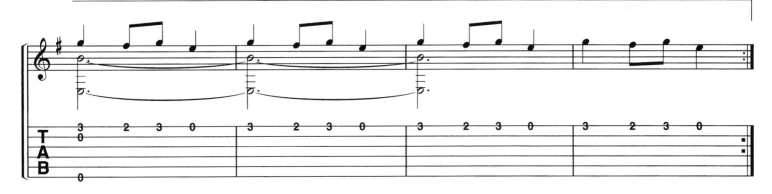

Ukrainian Carol - 2 - 2

UP ON THE HOUSETOP

Words and Music by
BENJAMIN RUSSELL HANBY

WE THREE KINGS OF ORIENT ARE

Words and Music by
JOHN H. HOPKINS, JR.

Verse 3:
Frankincense to offer have I,
Incense owns a deity nigh.
Prayer and praising, all men raising,
Worship Him, God most high.
(To Chorus:)

Verse 4:
Myrrh is mine: its bitter perfume
Breathes of life of gathering gloom;
Sorrowing, sighing, bleeding, dying,
Sealed in the stone cold tomb.
(To Chorus:)

Verse 5:
Glorious now behold Him arise;
King and God and sacrifice.
Alleluia, alleluia,
Earth to heaven replies.
(To Chorus:)

WE WISH YOU A MERRY CHRISTMAS

TRADITIONAL ENGLISH FOLK SONG

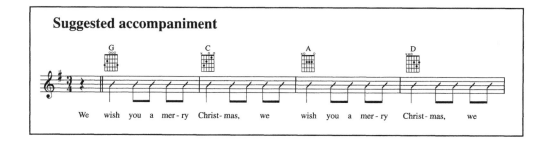

WHAT CHILD IS THIS?

Based on
GREENSLEEVES,
an Old English Air

By
WILLIAM C. DIX

Suggested accompaniment

1. What child is this who laid to rest on Mar - y's lap is sleep - ing?

Gently

1. What child is this___ who laid to rest___ on Mar - y's lap___ is
2. 3. *See additional lyrics*

sleep - ing? Whom an - gels greet___ with an - thems sweet,___ while

shep - herds watch___ are keep - ing? This, this___ is

Christ the King;___ Whom shep - herds guard___ and an - gels sing:

Haste, haste___ to bring Him laud,___ the Babe,___ the Son___ of Mar - y! 2. Why
3. So

Verse 2:
Why lies He in such mean estate,
Where ox and ass are feeding?
Good Christian, fear for sinners here,
The silent Word is pleading.
Nails, spears shall pierce Him through,
The cross be borne for me, for you.
Hail, hail the Word made flesh,
The Babe, the Son of Mary!

Verse 3:
So bring Him incense, gold, and myrrh,
Come peasant, King, to own Him;
The King of kings, salvation brings;
Let loving hearts enthrone Him.
Raise, raise the song on high,
The Virgin sings her lullaby.
Joy, joy, for Christ is born,
The Babe, the Son of Mary!

WINTER WONDERLAND

Words by
DICK SMITH

Music by
FELIX BERNARD

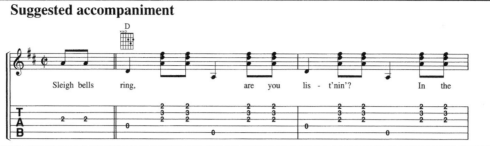

YOU'RE A MEAN ONE, MR. GRINCH

Lyrics by
DR. SEUSS

Music by
ALBERT HAGUE

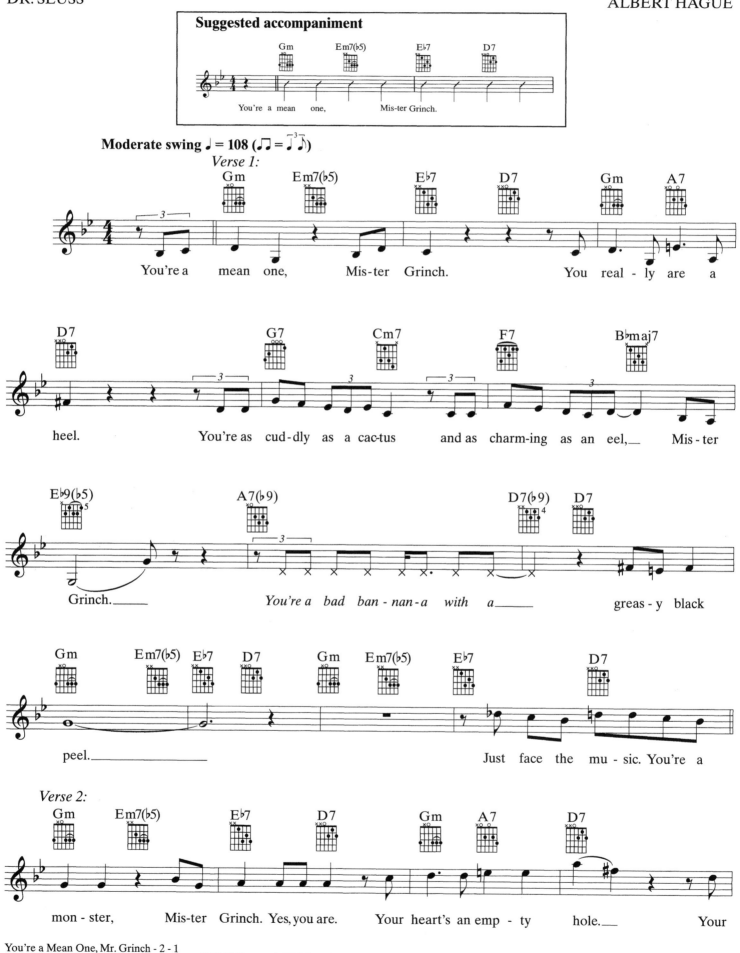

ANGELS WE HAVE HEARD ON HIGH

Traditional French Carol

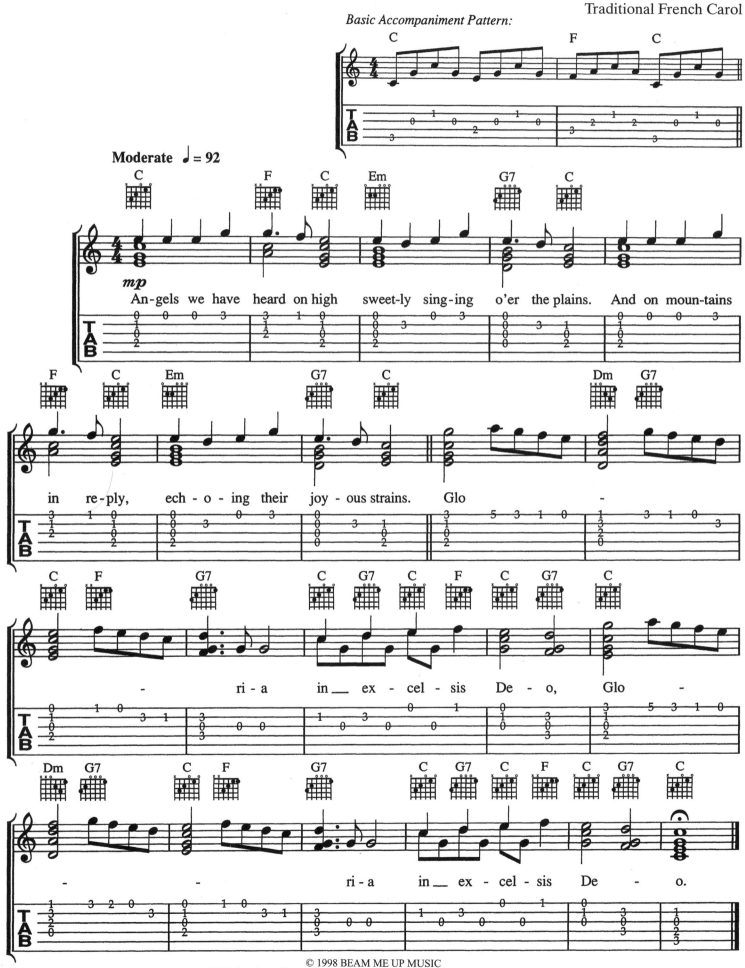

CANON IN D
("Pachelbel's Canon")

By JOHANN PACHELBEL
Arranged by SIMON SALZ

*Chord pattern repeats every four bars.

Canon in D - 3 - 1

Canon in D - 3 - 2

AVE MARIA

FRANZ SCHUBERT
Arranged by ALEXANDER GLÜKLIKH

Molto lento ♩ = 66 - 69

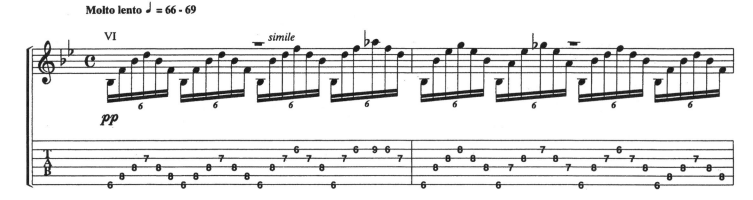

Ave Maria - 2 - 1

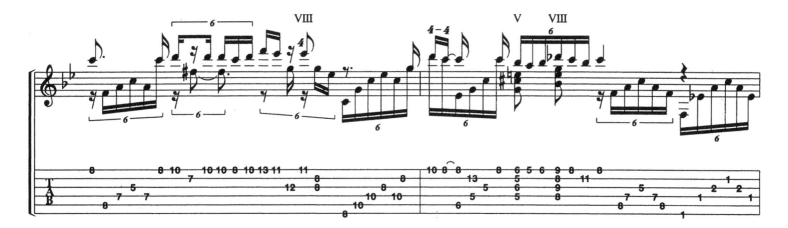

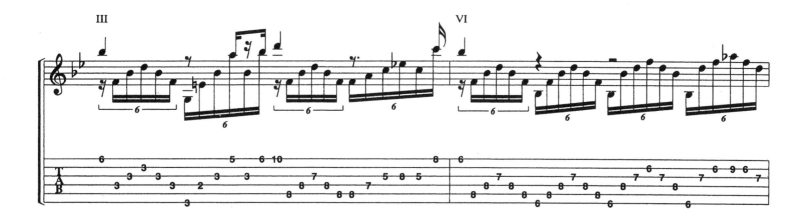

Ave Maria - 2 - 2

DECK THE HALL

Traditional Old Welsh

Performance Note: This is a very easy and full sounding arrangement. The notes with the stems going up are melody notes and the notes with stems going down are the accompaniment.

Deck the halls with boughs of hol - ly, fa la la la la la la la la.

'Tis the sea - son to be jol - ly, fa la la la la la la la la

Don we now our gay ap - par - el, fa la la, la la la la la la.

Troll the an - cient yule - tide car - ol, fa la la la la la la la la.

GRANDMA GOT RUN OVER
BY A REINDEER

Words and Music by
RANDY BROOKS

Performance Note: This arrangement is written in a country guitar style, with the melody in the bass. The grace note slurs that you see throughout the arrangement will give you a great country guitar effect. Play the grace note right on the beat, quickly hammering on to the next note.

Grand-ma got run o-ver by a rein-deer, walk-ing home from our house Christ-mas Eve. You can say there's no such thing as San-ta, but as for me and Grand-pa we be-lieve.

1. She'd been drink-ing too much
2.3. *See additional lyrics.*

Grandma Got Run Over by a Reindeer - 3 - 1

Verse 2:

Now we're all so proud of Grandpa,
He's been taking this so well.
See him in there watching football,
Drinking beer and playing cards with Cousin Mel.
It's not Christmas without Grandma.
All the family's dressed in black,
And we just can't help but wonder:
Should we open up her gifts or send them back?
(To Chorus:)

Verse 3:

Now the goose is on the table,
And the pudding made of fig,
And the blue and silver candles,
That would just have matched the hair in Grandma's wig.
I've warned all my friends and neighbors,
Better watch out for yourselves.
They should never give a license
To a man who drives a sleigh and plays with elves.
(To Chorus:)

GOD REST YE MERRY, GENTLEMEN

Traditional

Basic Accompaniment Pattern:

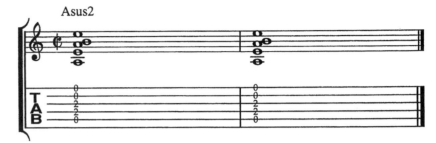

1. God rest you mer - ry, gen - tle - men, let noth - ing you dis - may. Re -
(2.) God our Heav'n-ly Fa - ther a bless - ed An - gel came, and

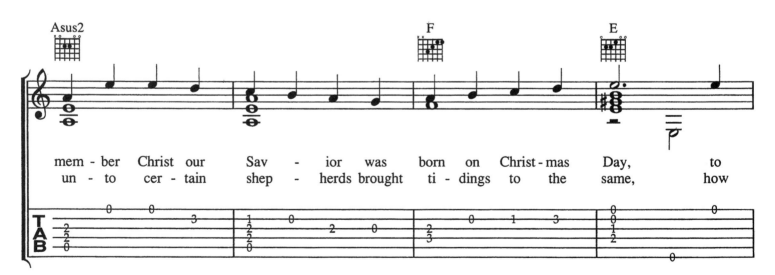

mem - ber Christ our Sav - ior was born on Christ - mas Day, to
un - to cer - tain shep - herds brought ti - dings to the same, how

God Rest Ye Merry, Gentlemen - 2 - 1

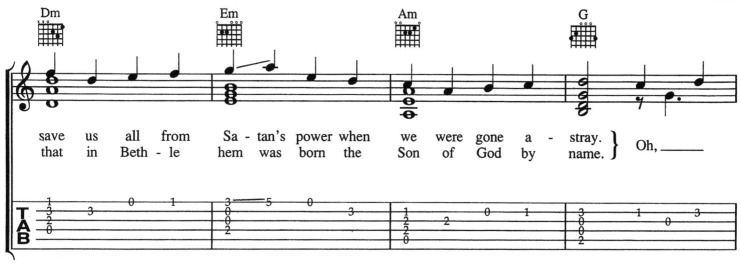

save us all from Sa - tan's power when we were gone a - stray. } Oh, _____
that in Beth - le hem was born the Son of God by name.

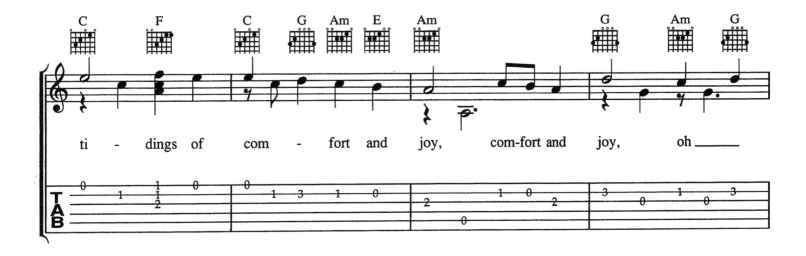

ti - dings of com - fort and joy, com-fort and joy, oh ____

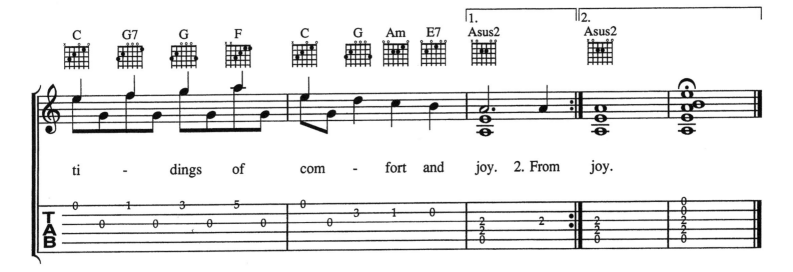

ti - dings of com - fort and joy. 2. From joy.

GREENSLEEVES

ANONYMOUS (16th Century)
Arranged by ALEXANDER GLÜKLIKH

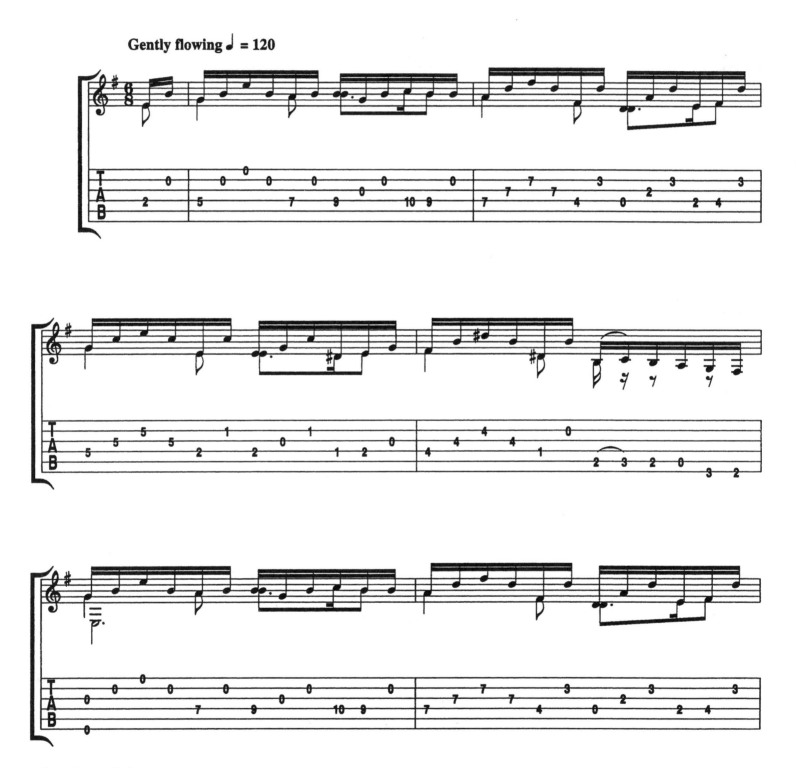

Greensleeves - 2 - 1

Greensleeves - 2 - 2

HAVE YOURSELF A
MERRY LITTLE CHRISTMAS

Words and Music by
HUGH MARTIN and
RALPH BLANE

Basic Accompaniment Pattern:

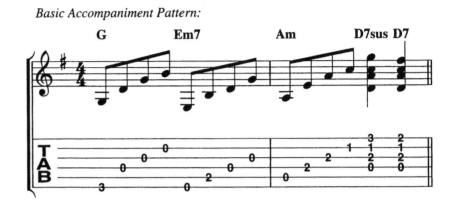

Verses 1 & 2:

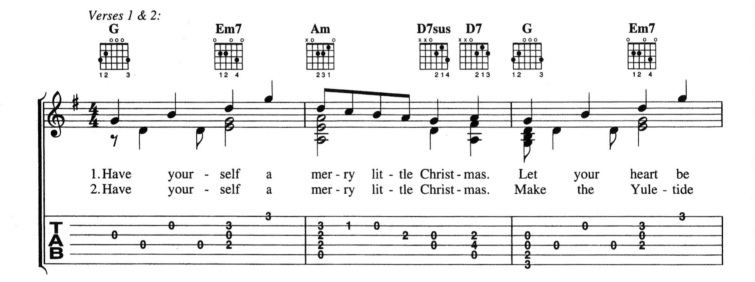

1. Have your - self a mer - ry lit - tle Christ - mas. Let your heart be
2. Have your - self a mer - ry lit - tle Christ - mas. Make the Yule - tide

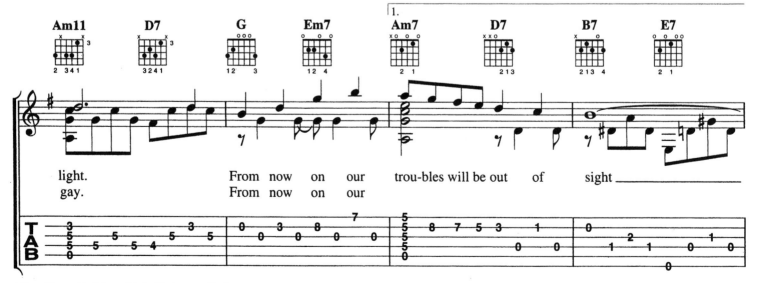

light. From now on our trou-bles will be out of sight
gay. From now on our

Have Yourself a Merry Little Christmas - 3 - 1

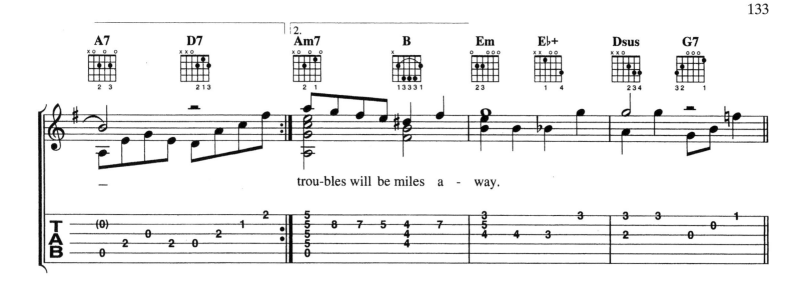

trou-bles will be miles a - way.

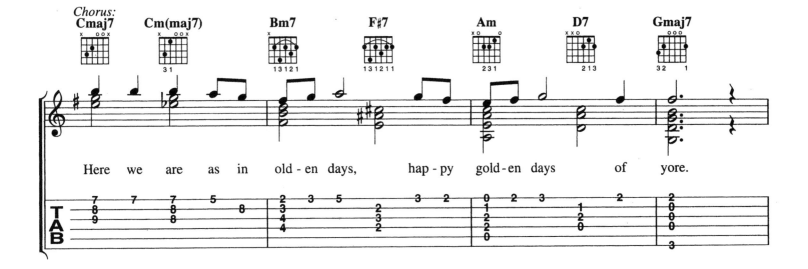

Chorus:

Here we are as in old - en days, hap - py gold - en days of yore.

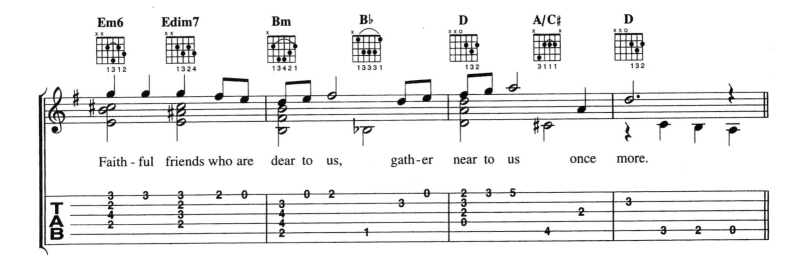

Faith - ful friends who are dear to us, gath - er near to us once more.

134

Verse 3:

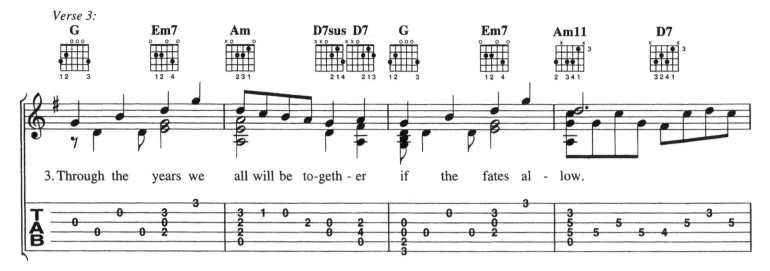

3. Through the years we all will be to-geth - er if the fates al - low.

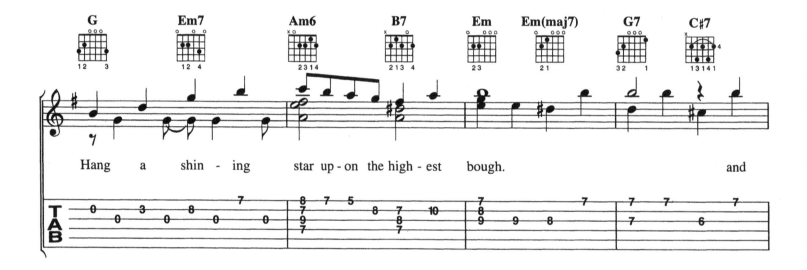

Hang a shin - ing star up - on the high - est bough. and

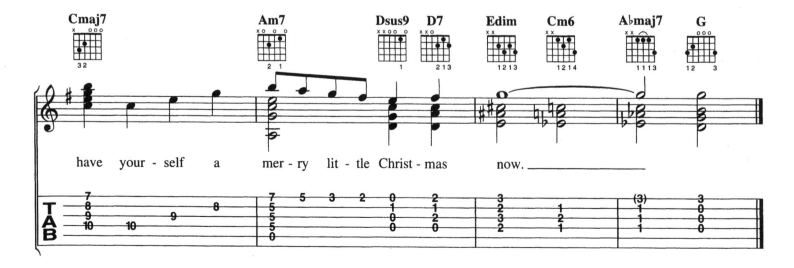

have your - self a mer - ry lit - tle Christ - mas now. _____

JINGLE BELLS

Words and Music by
J. PIERPONT

IT CAME UPON THE MIDNIGHT CLEAR

Words by RICHARD S. WILLIS
Music by EDMUND H. SEARS

Performance Note: This arrangement is a lot easier to play
than it looks. Remember that the notes with stems up are melody
notes and the notes with stems going down are the accompaniment.

Basic Accompaniment Pattern:

Andante ♪ = 108

1. It came up-on ___ the mid - night clear that
(2.) through the clo - ven skies they come with
3. *See additional lyrics.*

glo - rious song ___ of old, _____ from an - gels bend - ing
peace - ful wings ___ un - furled, _____ and still their heav - en - ly

near the earth to touch their harps ___ of gold. ___ Peace
mu - sic floats o'er all the wear - y world. ___ A -

It Came Upon the Midnight Clear - 2 - 1

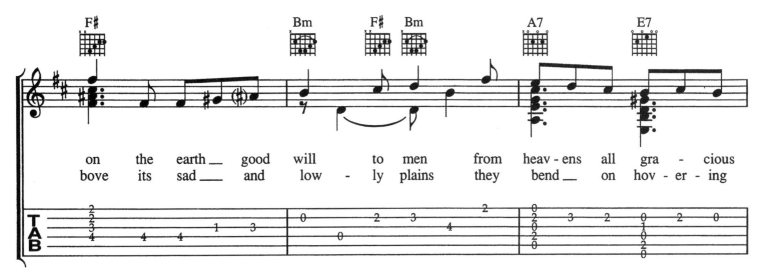

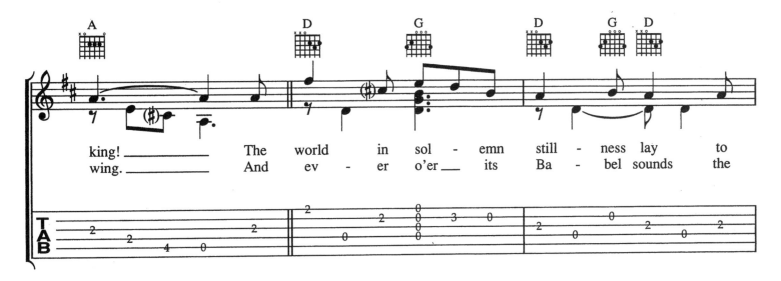

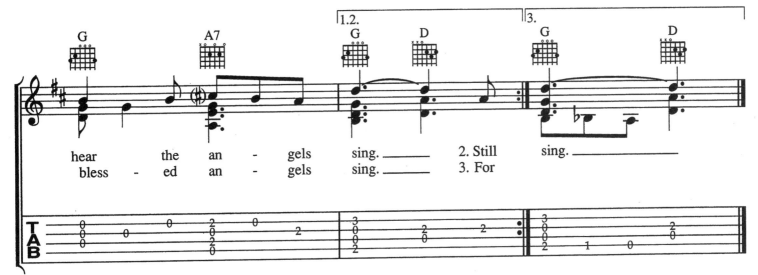

Verse 3:
For lo the days are hast'ning on.
By prophet bards foretold,
When with the ever circling years
Comes 'round the age of gold.
When peace shall over all the earth
Its ancient splendor fling.
And the whole world bring back the song
Which now the angels sing.

JESU, JOY OF MAN'S DESIRING

By
J. S. BACH

Jesu, Joy of Man's Desiring - 2 - 1

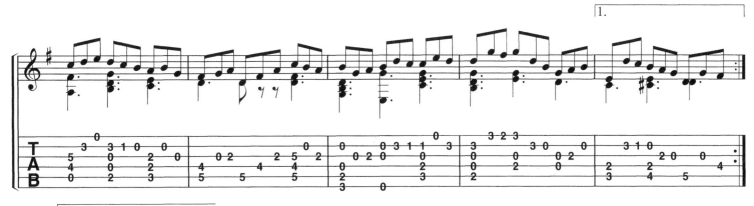

Jesu, Joy of Man's Desiring - 2 - 2

THE LITTLE DRUMMER BOY

Words and Music by
KATHERINE DAVIS, HENRY ONORATI
and HARRY SIMEONE

Basic Accompaniment Pattern:

Performance Note: The four measure introduction to this song is also used as an interlude. To get the right effect, finger each measure like a chord, then allow all notes to ring for the full measure. Pay particular attention to the accented notes. If allowed to ring, these notes form a separate melody.

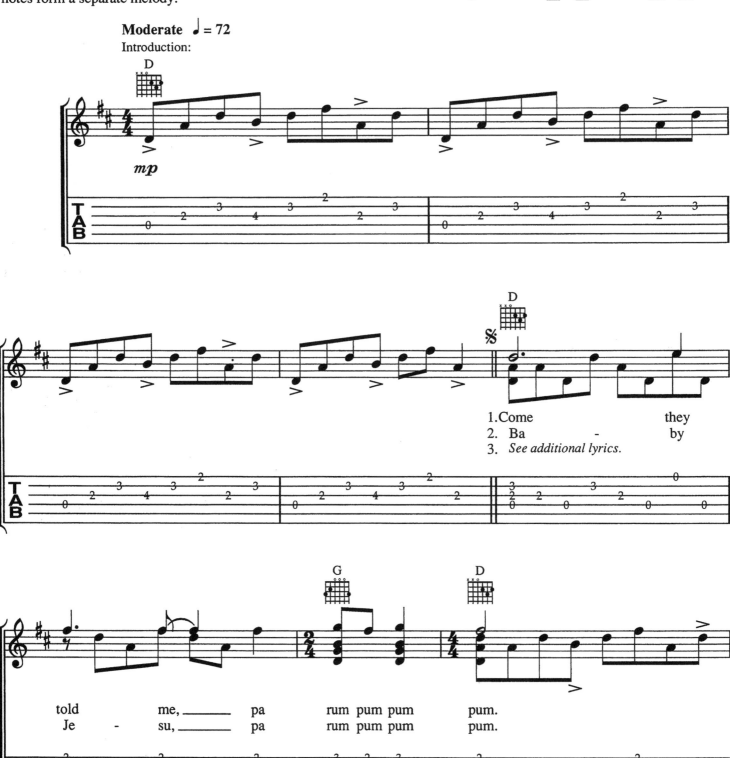

The Little Drummer Boy - 4 - 1

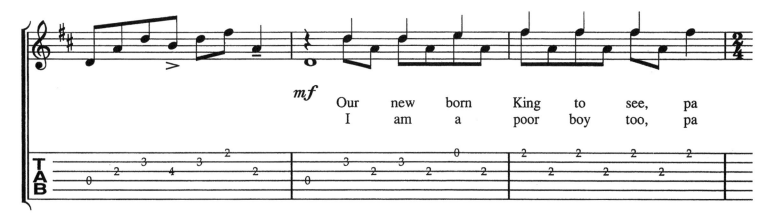

Our new born King to see, pa
I am a King poor boy too, pa

rum pum pum pum.
rum pum pum pum.

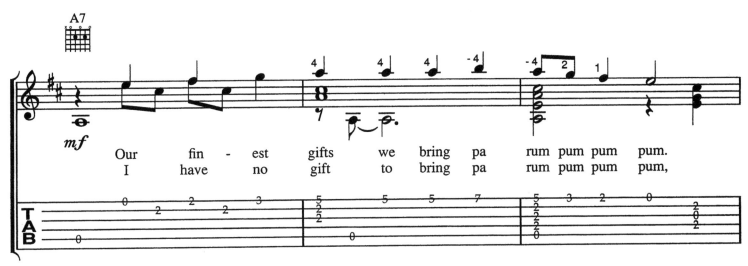

Our fin - est gifts we bring pa rum pum pum pum.
I have no gift to bring pa rum pum pum pum,

Our fin - est gifts we bring pa
that's fit to give our King pa

Let ring

The Little Drummer Boy - 4 - 2

142

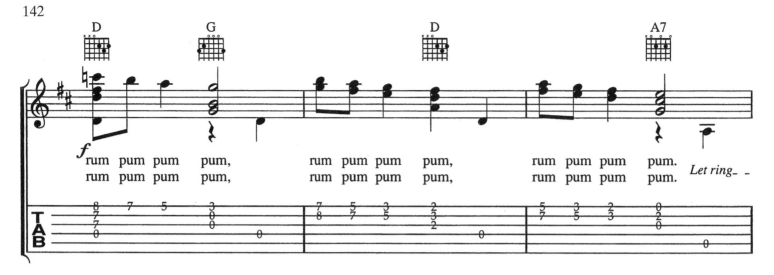

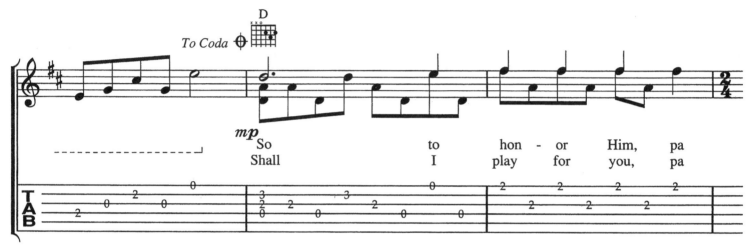

The Little Drummer Boy - 4 - 3

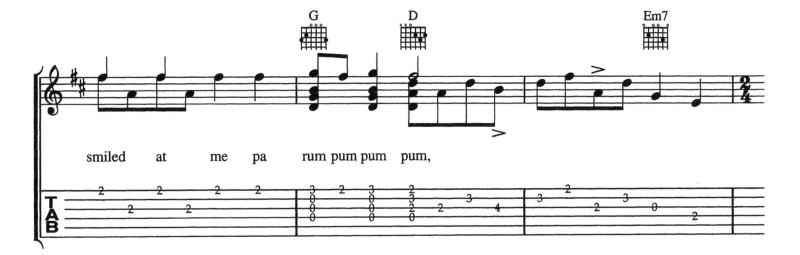

Verse 3:
Mary nodded
Pa rum pum pum pum.
The ox and lamb kept time
Pa rum pum pum pum.
I played my drum for Him,
Pa rum pum pum pum.
I played my best for Him,
Pa rum pum pum pum,
Rum pum pum pum,
Rum pum pum pum.
(To Coda)

O CHRISTMAS TREE
(O TANNENBAUM)

Old German Carol

Performance Note: This arrangement works best as a solo, which is why there is no suggested accompaniment part. Although this is probably the hardest arrangement in the book, with the aid of both the tablature and the chord block diagrams, it should be fairly easy to learn.

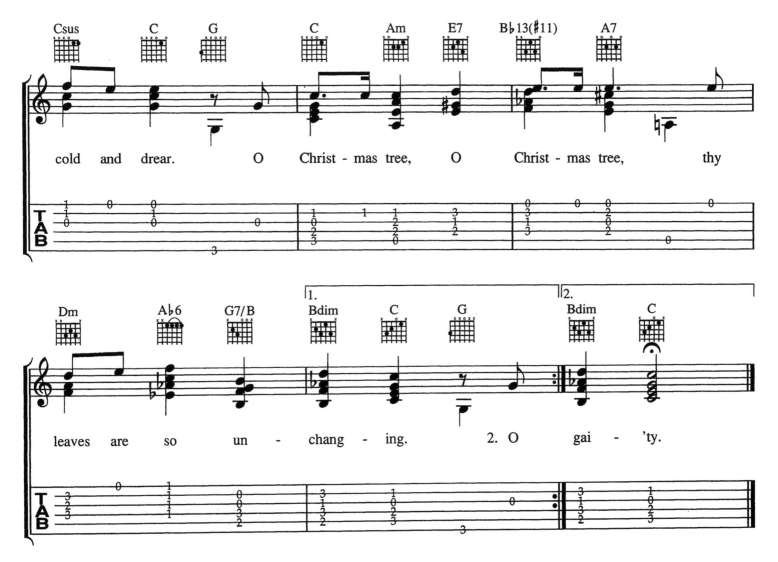

Verse 2:
O Christmas tree, O Christmas tree,
You fill all hearts with gai'ty.
O Christmas tree, O Christmas tree,
You fill all hearts with gai'ty.
On Christmas Day you stand so tall,
Affording joy to one and all.
O Christmas tree, O Christmas tree,
You fill all hearts with gai'ty.

German Lyric:
O Tannenbaum, O Tannenbaum,
Wie treu sind diene Bjätter.
O Tannenbaum, O Tannenbaum,
Wie treu sind diene Bjätter.
Du grunst nicht nur zur Sommer zeit,
Nein auch im Winter wenn es schneit.
O Tannenbaum, O Tannenbaum,
Wie treu sind diene Bjätter.

SILENT NIGHT

Words and Music by
JOSEPH MOHR and FRANZ GRUBER

Silent Night - 2 - 1

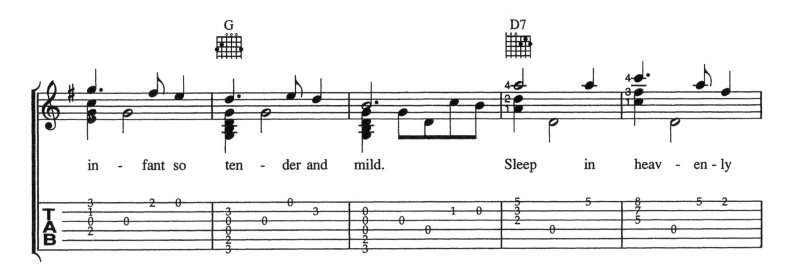

in - fant so ten - der and mild. Sleep in heav - en - ly

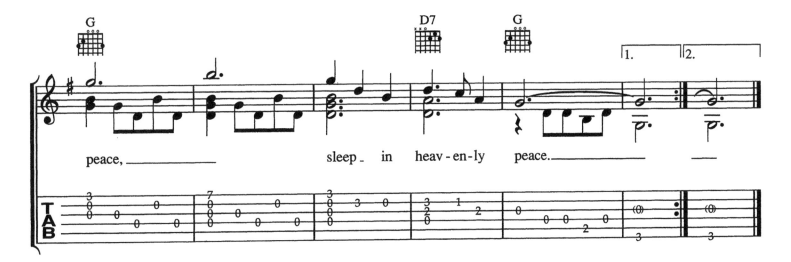

peace, _____ sleep _ in heav - en - ly peace. _____ ___

Verse 2:
Silent night, Holy night,
Shepherds quake
At the sight.
Glories stream from
Heaven afar,
Heavely hosts sing Alleluia,
Christ the Savior is born!
Christ the Savior is born!

WE THREE KINGS OF ORIENT ARE

Words and Music by
JOHN H. HOPKINS, JR.

Basic Accompaniment Pattern:

Moderate waltz ♩ = 120

Verse:

1. We three kings of O - ri - ent are, bear - ing
2.3.4. *See additional lyrics.*

gifts we tra - verse a - far, field and foun - tain,

moor and moun - tain, fol - low - ing yon - der star. O, _____

We Three Kings of Orient Are - 2 - 1

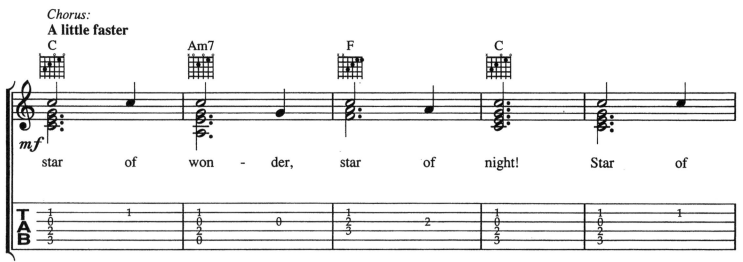

Verse 2:
Born a King on Bethlehem plain,
Gold I bring to crown Him again,
King forever ceasing never,
Over us all to reign.
(To Chorus:)

Verse 3:
Frankincense to offer have I,
Incense owns a Deity nigh;
Prayer and praising, all men raising,
Worship Him, God on high.
(To Chorus:)

Verse 4:
Myrrh is mine; its bitter perfume
Breathes a life of gathering gloom;
Sorrowing, sighing, bleeding, dying,
Sealed in the stone cold tomb.
(To Chorus:)

WHAT CHILD IS THIS?

Performance Note: This arrangement uses notes
on the first string, all the way up to the D at the 10th
fret. If you don't already know these notes, practice
the following exercise:

Based upon GREENSLEEVES
Old English Air
Lyrics by WILLIAM C. DIX

Basic Accompaniment Pattern:

What Child Is This? - 2 - 1

Verse 2:
Why lies He in such mean estate,
Where ox and ass are feeding?
Good Christian, fear for sinners here,
The silent Word is pleading.
Nails, spear shall pierce Him through,
The cross be borne for me, for you.
Hail, hail, the Word made flesh,
The Babe, the Son of Mary.

Verse 3:
So bring Him incense, gold and myrrh.
Come peasant, king, to own Him,
The King of kings salvation brings,
Let loving hearts enthrone Him.
Raise, raise the song on high,
The Virgin sings her lullaby;
Joy, joy for Christ is born,
The Babe, the Son of Mary.

What Child Is This? - 2 - 2

JOY TO THE WORLD

GEORGE F. HANDEL